DAYTRIPPER 4
50 Trips In Ontario Cottage Country

DAYTRIPPER 4

50 Trips In Ontario Cottage Country

Donna Gibbs Carpenter

The BOSTON
MILLS PRESS

APPRECIATION

My support system continues to function efficiently and effectively.
This book wouldn't have happened without the assistance of Stephen, Kaitlin,
Griffin, Mum and Dad; all worked above and beyond the call of duty.
John Denison, Noel Hudson, Kathy Fraser and Gill Stead are also due thanks.

CANADIAN CATALOGUING IN PUBLICATION DATA

Carpenter, Donna Gibbs, 1954-
Daytripper 4
Includes bibliographical refrences.
ISBN 1-55046-161-3

1. Ontario – Guidebooks. I. Title

FC3067.5.C37 1996   917.1304'4   C96-930314-9
F1057 C37 1996

Design by Gill Stead
Map Illustrations by Mary Firth

Printed in Canada
Cover photograph by John de Visser

First published in 1996 by
THE BOSTON MILLS PRESS
132 Main Street
Erin, Ontario, Canada
N0B 1T0
Tel 519-833-2407
Fax 519-833-2195

An affiliate of
Stoddart Publishing Co. Limited
34 Lesmill Road
North York, Ontario, Canada
M3B 2T6

The publisher gratefully acknowledges the support of
the Canada Council and Ontario Arts Council
in the development of writing and publishing in Canada.

CONTENTS

INTRODUCTION

We are so fortunate to live in Ontario. Adventures of every description lie around each bend in the road. *Daytripper* will open your eyes to places worth discovering, even though they may have existed right under your nose for years.

What is a daytrip? It's an outing lasting anywhere from a few hours to a full day. That means you can have an interesting and invigorating holiday and sleep in your own bed. It also means that the trips described in *Daytripper* are within a convenient distance of home, cottage, work, family and friends. Although the trips in this book are designed to be a day's length, that doesn't mean you can't string several of them together for a full holiday.

This volume of *Daytripper* covers cottage country, a vast region stretching from Lake Huron through Muskoka, Haliburton and the Kawarthas to the historic towns bordering Lake Ontario. Although the entire area is a magnet for vacationers, and has been for well over a century, it is by no means homogeneous. There are stretches of white sand along Lake Huron, sunken ships in the crystal clear waters of the Bruce Peninsula, and luxurious resorts on Lakes Joseph and Rosseau. While the wild and woolly backwoods of Haliburton are a part of cottage country, so too is the apple country of southern Georgian Bay, and the gentle currents of the Saugeen River. Cottage country daytripping is not only about the out-of-doors, as there are plenty of charming villages to visit for antique hunting, first-rate dining and polished museums.

The number of trips possible within cottage country is almost unlimited, but the best 50 have been carefully chosen. *Daytripper* has done the work of selecting the best natural and cultural features the region has to offer, and these are arranged as single-theme excursions. While each trip has a theme, it also includes several activities, so that each day is filled with variety. For example, a trip along the Lake Huron shore includes some time at the beach, a museum devoted to shipwrecks, a walk to the top of a lighthouse, and a lunch of fresh fish.

Daytripper is suitable for senior citizens, families of all ages, and single travellers. While many trips include a good walk or other exercise, this is not a book of rugged activities, and any of the trips can be tailored to the needs of a senior or toddler. These trips have been child tested; well-behaved children are welcome at all the sites mentioned.

Daytripper is not just for locals. It is also aimed at tourists looking for Ontario beyond the major attractions; it can be invaluable for showing off the province to visiting relatives and friends. Take it with you on business trips and to the cottage for things to do in your off-hours or on a rainy day.

There are a few things that daytrippers will not find in this book. Large, well-known attractions, such as amusement parks, will not be described. They are expensive and incompatible with the local culture and landscape. Most special events and festivals will not be described in *Daytripper*. The trips in this book are suitable over an extended season, not limited to only a week or two in the year. Any prearranged factory tours or other special-admission tours included in this book are those that are truly "visitor-friendly," since *Daytripper* adventures are meant to be spontaneous, and don't require a great deal of advance planning.

How to Use This Book

Keep it handy! You never know when you'll have a day free for an unplanned trip, so be prepared with *Daytripper* by the front door or in the glove compartment of your car.

Make sure you have an up-to-date, good-quality road map. The standard Government of Ontario highway map is very good, and the directions described in *Daytripper* assume that you have a map of at least this detail. Use the trip-finder on the following pages to identify trips within a close drive of home or trips that relate to your particular hobby or interest.

The season and hours of operation for museums and other attractions sometimes change, so if a trip includes a site of special interest to you, avoid disappointment by phoning ahead to check on hours of operation. This is especially good advice for holiday periods. Phone numbers are provided for those restaurants where reservations are recommended, or where a particular restaurant is a key element in a trip. Please also phone ahead to check on wheelchair accessibility and other special needs.

Most museums and other attractions charge an admission fee. In almost all cases this charge is very modest, considering the quality of the sites. You won't be disappointed. Some attractions, such as boat cruises, may cost a little more than a museum, but then they do offer a longer outing. The restaurants and inns suggested for daytrippers are average or inexpensive in price, unless otherwise noted. Some of the more costly locations may find a place within limited budgets at lunchtime.

Don't use *Daytripper* as the last word on adventure. Use it as a beginning, and feel free to go off discovering on your own. Ask questions of people you meet — shop owners, waiters and waitresses, and fellow travellers. Ontarians are pleased to tell of the special places within their own area. Follow their suggestions.

Have a good day!

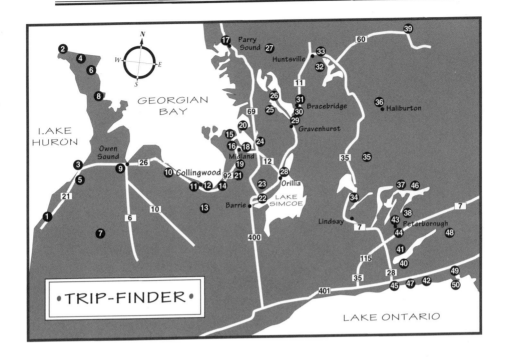

THE TRIP-FINDER

This trip-finder is an index to all 50 daytrips. It can be used in two ways. You can look up a topic of special interest and find the daytrip numbers listed. These numbers correspond to the number in large type at the beginning of each trip description. Or you can look up your home location and find the trips that are within a short distance (approximately 90 minutes) of home.

ACTIVITY TRIPS

HIKING, WALKING
2, 4, 6, 8, 11, 13, 14, 15, 19, 20, 21, 22, 27, 30, 31, 33, 36, 38, 39, 46, 50

FISHING
1, 2, 5, 10, 15, 36, 38, 39, 40

BIKING
8, 10, 12, 14, 15, 23, 27, 30, 36, 39, 50

WINTER SPORTS
9, 15, 19, 23, 33, 36, 39, 44

PLEASURE DRIVING
6, 7, 8, 10, 13, 24, 25, 32, 34, 35, 36, 37, 38, 40, 42, 48

SHOPPING
2, 3, 7, 10, 12, 13, 17, 19, 28, 30, 34, 37, 38, 42, 45, 46, 48, 49

BOATING, CRUISES, BOAT-WATCHING
1, 2, 5, 9, 10, 12, 14, 16, 17, 20, 22, 23, 24, 26, 28, 29, 30, 34, 35, 40, 43, 46, 47

SWIMMING
1, 2, 3, 4, 5, 11, 14, 15, 20, 22, 23, 38, 39, 41, 50

THEME TRIPS

HISTORY
1, 3, 7, 9, 10, 12, 14, 16, 17, 18, 20, 22, 24, 26, 27, 28, 29, 31, 32, 34, 35, 36, 38, 39, 40, 41, 42, 43, 44, 45, 46, 47, 48, 49, 50

NATURE
2, 4, 5, 6, 8, 10, 11, 13, 14, 15, 17, 19, 20, 21, 23, 25, 27, 33, 35, 36, 38, 39, 50

GARDENS
6, 21, 28, 43

THEATRE
1, 16, 28, 29, 34, 35, 43, 47

INDUSTRY & ENGINEERING
1, 3, 7, 10, 12, 13, 14, 24, 25, 29, 31, 34, 35, 41, 43, 48

CULTURAL HERITAGE
18, 41, 46

FARMING AND FARM MARKETS
7, 10, 21, 25, 48, 49

VISUAL ARTS, CRAFTS
2, 3, 5, 9, 10, 12, 13, 17, 19, 26, 28, 34, 35, 36, 37, 41, 45, 47, 48

HISTORIC INNS AND RESTAURANTS
1, 3, 7, 8, 10, 11, 12, 13, 24, 25, 26, 28, 29, 31, 32, 34, 35, 38, 40, 41, 45, 46, 47, 48

KIDS' TRIPS
1, 9, 11, 14, 15, 16, 18, 19, 20, 23, 27, 30, 33, 36, 38, 44, 50

TIMELY TRIPS

The following list suggests trips for those times when it can be difficult to find something to do.

WINTER
3, 9, 15, 19, 22, 23, 27, 32, 33, 36, 37, 39, 42, 44, 45, 47

RAINY DAYS
9, 12, 18, 26, 35, 37, 42, 45, 47

TRIPS BY LOCATIONS

These trips are within about a 90-minute drive of some of the larger cities and towns in Southern Ontario and cottage country.

OWEN SOUND
1, 2, 3, 4, 5, 6, 7, 8, 9, 10, 11, 12, 13, 14, 15, 16, 18, 19, 21, 22, 23

KITCHENER-WATERLOO, GUELPH
1, 3, 5, 7, 9, 10, 12, 13, 14, 21, 22, 23

TORONTO
10, 11, 12, 13, 14, 16, 18, 19, 21, 22, 23, 28, 38, 40, 41, 42, 43, 44, 45, 47, 49, 50

KINGSTON
47, 48, 49, 50

PETERBOROUGH
28, 34, 35, 36, 37, 38, 40, 41, 42, 43, 44, 45, 46, 47, 47, 48, 49, 50

BARRIE
9, 10, 11, 12, 13, 14, 15, 16, 17, 18, 19, 20, 21, 22, 23, 24, 25, 26, 27, 28, 29, 30, 31, 34, 35

HUNTSVILLE
16, 17, 18, 20, 24, 25, 26, 27, 28, 29, 30, 31, 32, 33, 35, 36, 39

PARRY SOUND
14, 15, 16, 17, 18, 19, 20, 21, 22, 23, 24, 25, 26, 27, 28, 29, 30, 31, 32, 33, 36, 39

BRACEBRIDGE
11, 12, 13, 14, 15, 16, 17, 18, 19, 20, 21, 22, 23, 24, 25, 26, 27, 28, 29, 30, 31, 32, 33, 34, 35, 36, 37, 38, 39

1 KINCARDINE
Beaches and Beacons

The Lake Huron shore has been loved by generations of vacationers. They come from Southwestern Ontario and Michigan to soak up the rays along kilometres of fine beaches, and race powerboats and yachts through the surf. Today's trip takes in two of the finest beaches, three lighthouses, and a treasure chest full of marine lore.

Point Clark juts out bravely into the lake between Goderich and Kincardine. It's best known for its 25-metre-tall and perfectly picturesque lighthouse, which has watched over these shores since 1859. To reach the light, exit Highway 21 at 2nd Line (Huron Road) and follow signs to Lighthouse Road. The light is at the end of this road; if you get wet, you've gone too far.

The lighthouse keeper's cottage is now a small museum with exhibits on the history of the light, local shipwrecks, and the lighthouse keepers of the past century. This is an "Imperial" lighthouse, circular in design, with stone walls a metre-and-a-half thick at the bottom and about half a metre thick at the top. An informative tour takes visitors to the tiptop for an eagle's-eye view of the region. This is not a tour for the acrophobic, however, since the top is entirely glass and the winding stairway is narrow, steep and open. But the view from the top is spectacular, with one crescent-shaped white beach after another stretched out along the coast in both directions. The lighthouse was built to warn ships away from a shoal about 3 kilometres offshore; you can see the shoal, marked by whitecaps and light blue water, from the lighthouse.

The view from the lighthouse will pique your curiosity about those lovely beaches, so drive north to visit a couple of them. You can meander along the lakeshore side roads or, for the fastest route, take Highway 21, with a stop at Pine River Cheese.

The first beach of the day is in Kincardine, 18 kilometres north of Point Clark. The strand is long and wide, and like most Huron beaches, has a narrow strip of pebbles at the waterline. Families tend to congregate at the south end of the beach, and the tan-and-muscle crowd sets up shop in the central area. There are change rooms, washrooms and a snack bar. An active marina is located at the north end of the beach, where charters are available for fisherfolk eager to land salmon, trout and pickerel.

An unusual, octagonal lighthouse dating to 1881 surveys the harbour from a prime hilltop location. The building is now a museum with displays on Kincardine's early years, when the harbour bustled with traffic in salt, grain and fish. Local shipwrecks are also documented. One of the best known is the *Erie Belle*, which sank in 1883 while pulling a sailing vessel off a sandy point south of town. The remains of the *Erie Belle* boiler can be seen from the 45-metre tower.

Just uphill from the lighthouse is the Erie Belle restaurant. It serves what may be the best fish and chips in Ontario, the fish fresh from the lake daily. The building is an old icehouse and warehouse that dates back to the days of sail.

Kincardine is known for its Scottish heritage, and on Saturday evenings during the summer, townspeople and visitors can follow a kilted piper to Victoria Park. Sunday afternoon and Wednesday evening concerts are held here as well. From July through early September the Bluewater Summer Playhouse presents comedies and musicals in the historic dance pavilion at the foot of Durham Street.

To sample a different Lake Huron beach, travel north on Highway 21 to Port Elgin. Port Elgin beach is for those who love summer as an endless round of beach volleyball and succumbing to the tempting aroma of beach burgers from several surfside vendors; the prevalent atmosphere is youthful. The beach is the location of summer carnivals, flea markets and Sunday evening concerts.

For those who prefer to be on or under the water, fishing charters and bait shops abound in Port Elgin, the surf is good for sail-boarding, and the clear waters of the lake make for excellent diving. Huron Kayak Adventure offers instruction, rentals and sales of coastal kayaks. Guided trips are available for the beginning or experienced paddler; the trips can include meals, and are a good way to explore lesser-known attractions along the coast.

Breakers crash against the rocks a couple of metres from the road along the scenic shore drive north from Port Elgin, past brilliant blue water, sailboats and several rocky islands. The largest of these is Chantry Island, with its much-photographed lighthouse, the last "light" of the day.

The Lake Huron shoreline provides for every interest, from sandcastles to sunset concerts. Discover Ontario's marine heritage and have a refreshing day outdoors at the same time.

Point Clark Lightkeeper's House
Mid-June–September:
Daily 11–5
(519) 395-3735

Kincardine Lighthouse and Museum
July–September:
Daily 12–5
Tuesday & Thursday 1–5
(519) 396-3150

Huron Kayak Adventure
(519) 389-5329

Bluewater Summer Playhouse
(519) 396-5722

2 TOBERMORY
Land's End, Ontario

Tiny Tobermory, at the very tip of the Bruce Peninsula, has a well-deserved reputation as a premier outdoors destination. It is the starting (or ending) point of the legendary Bruce Trail. Two harbours there shelter fishermen and yachters; divers seek the shipwrecks of Fathom Five National Park; and the town's quayside shops and restaurants are a delight for tourists. Tobermory is easy to find — just drive north on Highway 6 until you reach the water.

Outdoors enthusiasts hanker for the pleasures of the big water. Thousands of divers arrive in Tobermory annually to investigate Fathom Five National Marine Park, one of the first underwater national parks in the world. Its 21 shipwrecks, underwater caves and ancient coral reefs offer thrills to snorkellers and expert divers. Dive equipment, lessons and transportation are available from several locations in town, and local motels provide package vacations of rooms, breakfast and oxygen. The national park visitor centre in town is a good source of information on dive-site conditions and regulations.

Landlubbers will want to drive to Big Tub Harbour and park at Lighthouse Point to watch divers enter the water. (Tobermory has been known as Tub since the early 1800s, and its twin harbours are known as Big Tub and Little Tub.) On the open side of the point, water foams against the rocky shoreline under the shadow of the classic red and white lighthouse (1885). The water in this region is famous for its clarity, and in the sheltered bay you can get a good look at the way the limestone bottom is deeply fissured into large blocks.

Sea kayaking is an increasingly popular way to explore the tip of the Bruce and the many beautiful and protected inlets of the 19 islands of Fathom Five. Rentals and information are available in Little Tub Harbour.

One of the best ways to appreciate the unique features of Fathom Five is to take one of the glass-bottom boat tours that operate from Little Tub Harbour. Select the one that best fits your schedule. Tours begin with Big Tub Harbour and two shipwrecks, the *Sweepstakes* (a 36-metre, two-masted schooner abandoned here in 1885) and the City of Grand Rapids (a 37-metre steamer that burned and sank in 1907). Because the wrecks are in shallow water, the mast holes, deck hatches and centreboard of *Sweepstakes* are easily visible, as are the burned engine and ribs of the Grand Rapids.

 After the shipwrecks, tours travel to fabulous Flowerpot Island, named for two huge examples of the weird rock columns found along the Bruce Peninsula. Flowerpots are created when waves erode the soft lower limestone along the shoreline and leave the broad, hard dolomite upper rock; the entire formation is shaped like a flowerpot. Flowerpot Island's rugged appeal comes from its unusual towering orange cliffs, its caves and lush forest, a historic lighthouse, Canada's oldest living tree (a 1,645-year-old cedar), gargantuan (but elusive) toads, and orchids. Almost all of the peninsula's 41 species of orchid thrive here in the mild and moist island climate, including the rare calypso orchid, a fragile pink, white and yellow belle that is found down at ankle height. Island orchids are not to be disturbed! One popular daytrip is to disembark at Flowerpot Island and return on a later tour boat (arrange for pickup when purchasing a ticket); this allows several hours for the trails, caves and boulder beaches.

Don't think that the attractions of Tobermory are only out on the water. The town itself — a colourful little village hugging the steep sides of a rocky inlet — is enchanting. The harbour is abustle with yachters and cruisers seeking shelter and supplies. Tobermory is still an active commercial fishery, and there are usually a couple of "turtleback" fishing tugs at the wharf, where you can purchase fresh and smoked whitefish. The Chi-Cheemaun

 Ferry, which travels to Manitoulin Island daily from May to October, unloads at its own wharf.

Tobermory has several restaurants that serve local whitefish. Perhaps the most unusual is minuscule Craigie's, a fish-and-chippery active since 1920 — the fresh fish, worn wooden floors, and view of the harbour make Craigie's worth a visit.

You may have noticed the signs all along Highway 6: Tobermory is the location of the Sweet Shop, which dispenses old-fashioned candies as well as premium ice creams. There are two good art shops in town, the Golden Gallery and Circle Arts. The former is the best place for paintings of the lovely Bruce scenery that delights newcomer and seasoned visitor alike. Circle Arts has a splendid collection of pottery, blown glass, carved wooden bowls, sculpture and collage from local artists. There are too many smaller shops to mention by name, but rest assured that whether you are looking for nautical clothing, books, or supplies, Tobermory can supply them in abundance.

Tobermory is one of Ontario's treasures, windswept and wild, but with plenty of small-town charm as well. The "Tip of the Bruce" may well be the best of the Bruce.

Fathom Five National Marine Park
(519) 596-2233

Seaview III Boat Tours
(519) 596-2950

Great Blue Heron Boat Tours
(519) 596-2250

True North Boat Tours
(519) 596-2600

3 SOUTHAMPTON
Ontario's Brigadoon

Southampton is a Lake Huron resort town that retains the dig-nity of summers long ago — stately homes and yachts, carriage rides and lawn bowling. The town is a bit of a Brigadoon, a door-way to a pleasant day in the nineteenth century.

Gain a vivid sense of the past on Victoria Street at the Bruce County Museum, housed in an 1878 schoolhouse. (Look for directional signs throughout town.) There are few local history museums that can touch the quality of this one, with its broad range of artifacts, spacious layout, and profes-sionally arranged exhibits. Our trip to the nineteenth century begins at the replica of a small-town street, with a watch and clock maker, a dressmaker and McVittie's General Store.

There are also exhibits on aboriginal people, farming, forestry, the railways and the RCMP. Don't miss the maritime room on the top floor. A huge amount of information is presented by way of maps, model ships, and nautical equipment — from barrels to captain's logbooks. Local shipwrecks, Southampton shipbuilding, Huron coastal canoes, the fishing industry and Great Lakes ship-ping — all are explored here; the romance and danger of our great inland sea fills the room.

The museum's holdings include 2,000 photographs by local John Scougall that lovingly capture life in a small coastal town at the turn of the century. When you exit the museum, take a look around at the historic homes and tree-lined streets. You might hear the clink of the bowls at the lawn-bowling club. It is as if you have entered one of the sepia photographs of the past. Southampton has apparently survived the rav-ages of time with grace.

The museum provides a walking-tour brochure on Southampton's historic buildings. Read it as you walk west along Lansdowne Street toward the lake. At Huron Street turn right (north) to find a snug harbour and an 1887 lighthouse. The harbour may be popular with recreational boaters, but it is also a working harbour where about 50 people are employed in the fishing industry.

Walk south to High Street, the broad main street, and turn toward Southampton's lovely beach. The broad, white beach is uncrowded even on a summer weekend, and has a good view of the Chantry Island lighthouse. If you still have legs left, walk along High Street to Huron and turn south (right). There are several attractive homes in the next couple of blocks, most built in the mid-1800s for lighthouse keepers, fishermen and marine merchants.

Return to High Street, where there are many restaurants to choose from. Two of them are particularly suitable for our historic theme of the day. The Walker House has served home cooking for about 140 years. The atmosphere is small-town friendly; the menu features Lake Huron whitefish, pickerel and trout, and on weekends there is a popular hip-of-beef buffet. The Chantry House Inn may be identified by its colourful perennial garden. The dining room is intended mainly for guests, so reservations for visitors are essential. Many of the Pennsylvania Dutch recipes used at the inn have been in the owner's family for hundreds of years; specialties include Russian Mennonite stroganoff, smoked pork chop, and rouladen with sausage.

Stroll along High Street in the direction of the museum. You may want to visit antique and gift shops such as Bayberry's and Just Browsing. Follow your nose to the Offshore Bakery. Fans of healthy eating will love the breads; Swiss grain, Winnipeg rye, muesli and sourdough are just a few of the fragrant choices. Those with a sweet tooth will want to sample "Bruce County's best butter tarts," chocolate-chunk macadamia cookies, or apple-berry cheesecake.

When you are ready to reenter the twentieth century, pick up the car near the museum and head south along Albert Street (Highway 21). At the south end of town in an old industrial building is the Southampton Market, part farm market, part flea market, where bargain hunters will find piles of lunch boxes, burner savers, sweat suits, steel wool, craft supplies and stamp pads, and other treasures. Much of the building is devoted to reproduction furniture — dining and occasional tables, chairs, bookcases and beds. It's a terrific place to find anything you need to put together your own country furniture, with room after cavernous room of chair legs, headboards, tabletops, drawer slides, hinges and sandpaper.

Continue out of town on Highway 21. There are two good ways to take a bit of Southampton home with you. Inland Sea Products sells fresh and smoked whitefish, trout, herring, perch and pickerel. And you can visit Creative Fields, further south in the Castle Village shopping mall, for the paintings of local artists.

The good thing about Southampton — unlike Brigadoon — is that we can take pleasure in its loveliness whenever we need a respite from the twentieth century.

Bruce County Museum and Archives
Monday–Friday 9–5
Sunday 1–5
May–September only:
Saturday 9–5
(519) 797-3644

Chantry House Inn
(519) 797-2646

4 BRUCE PENINSULA NATIONAL PARK
Wuthering Heights

The Niagara Escarpment is many things to many people. To the photographer, the Escarpment is a scenic wonder of grey cliff and crystalline waters; for the botanist it is a treasure trove of orchids, ferns and ancient cedars; to the rock climber it is a place for exploring great depths and soaring heights. In 1990 the Escarpment was designated a World Biosphere Reserve by the United Nations, which indicates that the region is as precious as the Galapagos Islands and the Serengeti Plains.

The Escarpment may be best appreciated through the trails and facilities of Bruce Peninsula National Park. The main entrance is just east of Highway 6 in the northern section of the peninsula. Stop at the gatehouse to pick up a copy of the informative park newspaper and a trail map. Drive to the parking lots near the "Head of Trails" where several trails fan out.

The most recommended route is a 3-kilometre loop that combines portions of the Georgian Bay and Marr Lake Trails; it also follows part of the Bruce Trail (marked with white paint on trees and rocks). Walk north from where the Georgian Bay Trail meets the water to Halfway Point Rock and a dramatic vista of a grey, craggy rock wall that plunges into the shimmering, turquoise water. (Hang on to any adventurous youngsters!) The rugged wall of rock is uninterrupted for many kilometres in both directions; it reaches up to 40 metres in height, and plummets to 200 metres below the water's surface. Although deep, the water is remarkably clear, and reveals every crack and crevice in the limestone slabs. The upper layer of rock on which you perch is hard dolomite and the under layers are softer limestone; the pounding waves erode the limestone more quickly than the dolomite, which explains why so many cliffs have overhangs. The limestone is deeply fissured, and these nooks and crannies are home to turkey vultures, ravens, swallows and bats.

Take a look at the plant life, large and very small, that ekes out a living from the rock. The stunted, twisted cedars that cling precariously to the precipice are Canada's oldest trees. Scientists have made this discovery rather recently, dating some Bruce Peninsula old-timers to more than 1,600 years ago. Because of their inaccessibility and stunted size, these trees have been spared the forester's axe that devastated much of the upland forest in the region. Look closely at the rocks under your feet. They are covered with plants — grey, green and orange mosses, lichens and tiny, curly ferns — that somehow manage to thrive in an environment of fierce winds, unrelenting sun, rock falls and foot traffic. Another unusual fact of Bruce Peninsula botany is that there are tiny plant forms, called cryptoendolithic life, that actually live inside the rocks. The Bruce Peninsula is one of the few locations on Earth where this phenomenon occurs.

Just north of Halfway Point Rock the trail reaches Indian Head Cove, a good place to see divers as they enter the water to explore underwater caves. One of these caves, the Grotto, also has a land entrance; it provides a convenient frame for photographs of Georgian Bay. The cove is also popular with swimmers, although the water in the park's Cyprus Lake is much warmer. You can continue along on the Bruce Trail until Overhanging Point and another overlook, or return along the Marr Lake Trail. This latter route crosses a boulder field that stretches from the beach well back into the forest. You'll scramble over white boulders of remarkably uniform size and shape, worn smooth by years of pounding surf.

The trail enters refreshingly cool cedar and balsam fir woodlands to end up at the Head of Trails. Be on the lookout through the woods for some of the park's 1,250 species of plants, which include 20 ferns, 41 orchids and 5 species of insect-eating plants. White-tailed deer, porcupine, bats and raccoons are common, and although the endangered massasauga rattler is a denizen of the park, it is rarely encountered. Cyprus Lake flows out here as a pretty little stream crossed by way of a log bridge.

For those who want a less demanding walk, there is the 1-kilometre Cyprus Lake Trail, which skirts the lakeshore. On a hot day, its two beaches are welcome places to cool off. The 1-kilometre Horse Lake Trail traverses a good many habitat types, such as marsh, woods and boulder beach, in a walk of moderate difficulty. Park staff run a full interpretive program all summer long. Hike to Lord Hunt's Tunnel, Cliff Hangers, and Rock Ramble are some of the intriguing names given to the planned activities.

The Niagara Escarpment is one of the world's truly special places, a scenic wonder with a biological diversity rarely found elsewhere. Celebrate your good fortune in having such a place on your doorstep by taking a walk along Ontario's wuthering heights.

Bruce Peninsula National Park
Open daily year-round
(519) 596-2263

5 PAISLEY
Paddle with the Pioneers

A heron, one leg poised, scans the brown water for prey; mergansers lift from the water; and a few paddle strokes brings your canoe in line with the best course through the upcoming rapids. Scenes from the diary of an early pioneer? No, this is contemporary Ontario, and the pleasure of paddling through unspoiled countryside just as the pioneers did belongs to travellers in those parts of Bruce and Grey Counties called Saugeen Country.

This region of serene family farms and nineteenth-century villages has as its heart the Saugeen River, which runs 100 kilometres from Hanover to Lake Huron. The Saugeen has a reputation among canoeists as the best family (read beginner) river in Southern Ontario because of its deep pools, beginner-level rapids, and short portages. There are several access points, and you can canoe the entire length, or have a shorter outing from Walkerton to Paisley or from Paisley to Southampton. Today's trip takes advantage of the services of Cowan's Canoes in Paisley (located in central Bruce County), and travels from that town to Southampton.

Paisley was a booming railway and industrial town a century ago, and to the credit of heritage-minded citizens, its main street retains the ambience of small-town, rural Ontario. You may want to make an exploration of Paisley, just as the pioneers would have, before setting out on the Saugeen. At the centre of town are the town hall (1876) and the landmark green tower of the fire hall (1891). Across the street from these two fine buildings are two mills dating to the same period.

Paisley has several interesting stores to call upon, most along Queen Street. Antique hunters will love the Vault Door. Whether you're looking for a grain scale, a butter box, or a piece of Depression glass, this store is for you.

Just across the street is the Incidental Shop and Tea Room, the best place to fatten the picnic hamper with some homemade tarts, Irish cream cheesecake, or apple dumplings.

Several appealing shops are located on Queen Street just north of the river. There's the Saugeen Studio (ceramics), the Macnamara Gallery (goldsmithing), Cover to Cover (used books), and the Elora Soap Company (handmade soaps such as witch hazel and oatmeal-tangerine). Across the street is the Treasure Chest Museum. Local Norman Hagedorn, collector extraordinaire, left this private museum to the people of Paisley. There are two floors of neatly displayed agricultural implements, coin and stamp collections, and an array of household items — from copper kettles to over 150 wash jugs and basins.

Also on Queen Street near the river is Cowan's Canoes, the main attraction of the day. Cowan's, open daily during the canoeing season, rents several types of canoes, paddles and lifejackets, and provides a shuttle service that picks up paddlers at prearranged locations and times. It's a good idea to phone ahead to book the equipment and shuttle, and to check on expected weather and water conditions. (High spring run-off can change easy ripples into challenging rapids. In late summer the Saugeen can be low and slow; voyageurs may want to wait until prime fall conditions.) One inconvenience our ancestors would not have had to cope with is the crowded conditions on the river during the Victoria Day weekend — and the wise paddler avoids the river during those three days.

Although Saugeen is farm country, the steep banks of the river are forested, sheltering river travellers in a quiet and remote world populated with ducks, heron, kingfishers, muskrat and beaver. Cast a line here for bass, pike and trout. There are many sections of rapids, although these are easily managed and of short duration.

High clay banks rise to 30 metres at the Saugeen Bluffs Conservation Area, a convenient picnic spot. This park offers picnic sites, washrooms, drinking water, and a high vista of the river. Downstream of the conservation area, the river loses its high banks, and widens and branches into several channels divided by treed islands. The trip ends at the rendezvous point, Denny's Dam near Southampton. It's easy to gauge your progress according to the bridges encountered on today's trip. Each bridge (not counting the first one) marks one quarter of your voyage. A typical paddle from Paisley to Southampton will take about six hours, and those seeking a shorter outing can arrange to be picked up at any of the bridges.

Paddle in the wake of the pioneers and keep company with kingfishers and wildflowers. Just part of a typical day in Saugeen Country.

Cowan Canoes
(519) 353-5535

Treasure Chest Museum
July & August:
Daily 11–5
May, June, September:
Saturday & Sunday 11–5
(519) 353-5109

6 DYER'S BAY
Florabundance

The Bruce Peninsula is wealthy in floral beauty. The region has several habitat types, such as wet fen, and supports an unusual assortment of plants. Forests and meadows are habitat for 43 of Ontario's 60 species of orchids. But you don't have to be a botanist to appreciate this special environment, as the following flower-power tour illustrates.

The Singing Sands and Dorcas Bay Nature Preserve are located about 15 kilometres south of Tobermory, west off Highway 6. The route is signposted for Singing Sands, a 15-kilometre beach named for the eerie sound the wind makes as it sweeps across the sand. Even when it is stifling hot elsewhere, the beach at Dorcas Bay is often shrouded in a light fog that lends a surreal look to beach umbrellas and wading children.

Dorcas Bay Nature Preserve borders the north side of Singing Sands. The preserve is owned by the Federation of Ontario Naturalists, and the federation generously keeps this preserve open to the public. In return, the public is expected to keep to pathways, "taking only photographs, leaving only footprints."

Dorcas Bay is remarkable in its diversity. It has dry and wet sand dunes, rocky barrens and forest. In late June and early July there are bright masses of yellow lady's-slipper, showy lady's-slipper, the dainty rose pogonia, and fragrant white bog orchid. You'll also encounter photographers with enormous lenses on their cameras, reflective foil, and other equipment used to create a perfect floral photo.

As you drive to the next stop, you may think that you are being followed by an entourage of out-of-province cars; that is because the Bruce's floral wonders attract botanists from far and wide who tend to visit the same places. Drive south on Highway 6 and turn east on the Dyer's Bay road. When you reach the checkerboard sign at a T-intersection, head left and follow signs to Larkwhistle, where the forces of nature have been directed by human creativity (and buckets of hard labour) to create scenes of floral grace. Larkwhistle is the home of Patrick Lima and John Scanlon. Lima is one of Canada's most accomplished garden writers, with a handsome collection of books on perennials, herbs and kitchen gardens to his credit. Scanlon's photographs have accompanied some of Lima's writing. There is a modest charge for entry, and you are asked to respect the scheduled visiting hours.

A tour of the garden is aided by the purchase of a small guidebook that identifies plants and describes the guiding philosophy behind the garden design. There are the borders: iris, rose, perennial and yellow. There are the peony and old rose gardens (the potent fragrance harkens back to grandfather's garden), and the kitchen and herb gardens. Larkwhistle uses some familiar plants in successful new ways: look for mullein (more commonly seen in old cattle pastures) rubbing shoulders with iris, lilies, yarrow and creeping thyme. The garden has seven raised concrete pools that may appear strictly ornamental but provide a much-needed water supply for a garden that operates without water pressure and hoses, since Larkwhistle has no conventional electricity.

The quiet garden is Larkwhistle's newest addition, and may be the favourite of visitors. (Although Larkwhistle is one of those places that wherever you are standing is the best part of all.) Foliage plants take centre stage in the quiet garden, and along with the expected hosta and iris are geranium, sea lyme grass, and lady's mantle — an old favourite at its finest when raindrops or dew decorate the leaves. Colour is provided by delphiniums, phlox, lilies and clematis.

Larkwhistle's healthy, organically grown plants attract many visitors, both human and non: bees and butterflies happily

 flit from bee balm to squash, and a house wren chatters away from a shrub in the kitchen garden. Larkwhistle has earned a well-deserved reputation among the green-thumb set.

The last floral sojourn is Petrel Point, another pre-serve of the Federation of Ontario Naturalists. Drive south on Highway 6 and turn west toward Red Bay (the turn is just south of Mar). At Red Bay turn north and follow signs for Petrel Point. Although Petrel Point is tiny, only about 12 hectares, its two trails merit exploration. This is a wet fen; this low, damp place is not filled with cattails, but with the carnivorous sun-dew and pitcher plants. This is a nutrient-poor ecosystem, and car-nivorous plants make up for a lack of soil nitrogen by feeding on insects. The pitcher plant is common at Petrel Point. It's the one with the red-and-green cup-shaped leaves at the base and a nod-ding flower head supported on a spindly stalk. The cups fill with water and trap unsuspecting bugs, which are then at the mercy of plant digestive juices. It is these plants, along with small clumps of

black spruce and a cedar-tamarack forest, that make Petrel Point a landscape you are unlikely to see any-where else in Ontario.

Any time from late March to October the Bruce Peninsula has some interesting plant to seek out, whether a field of Ohio golden-rod or a single fragile orchid. Come and enjoy the Bruce in all its florabundance.

Larkwhistle Gardens
Saturday & Sunday 10–4
Wednesday 1–4
(800) 265-3127

Dorcas Bay, Singing Sands, Petrel Point
Daily, year-round

7 NEUSTADT
Town and Country

Although southern Bruce and Grey Counties may not be considered cottage country, vacationers who journey through this region en route to Lake Huron should take the time to appreciate its fine backroad driving and crossroads hamlets.

Begin the day in Neustadt, located on County Road 10 just south of Hanover. Neustadt's main street curves past the remarkable Huether Brewery, a massive stone building dating to 1869, and famous for its underground storage caverns. Many of the town's notable buildings, such as St. Peter's Church, the Neustadt Tavern, and the public library, date to the 1860s. Ask locals for directions to the childhood home of John Diefenbaker on Barbara Street.

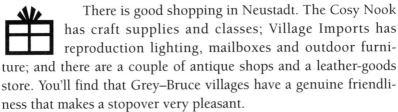

There is good shopping in Neustadt. The Cosy Nook has craft supplies and classes; Village Imports has reproduction lighting, mailboxes and outdoor furniture; and there are a couple of antique shops and a leather-goods store. You'll find that Grey–Bruce villages have a genuine friendliness that makes a stopover very pleasant.

From Neustadt, drive west on Road 16 and south on Highway 9 to Mildmay. At the north end of town is popular Mildmay–Carrick Conservation Area, with swimming and picnicking facilities. The 1876 Commercial Hotel sits at the centre of town; it's not hard to imagine stagecoaches drawing up in front of this venerable stone building. The Mildmay Creamery sells plenty of high-quality cheeses, including products from local Pine River and Teeswater dairies.

From Mildmay, drive west on County Road 24 and north on County Road 12. This is the heart of Ontario's cattle country; Bruce and Grey Counties are the largest producers of beef and hay in the province. The neat-as-a-pin farms are obviously prosperous, and many proudly display their name and specialty, whether cattle, sheep, draft horses or milk.

A steep hill leads down to Formosa, which, like most rural villages, can be identified from a distance by a tall steeple. Formosa's church, Immaculate Conception, is particularly dominant, with its 60-metre spire and seating for almost a thousand. Formosa Springs Brewery has satisfied knowledgeable quaffers since 1870. Now named Algonquin Brewing, it continues to produce quality beverages using on-site spring water. The brewery store sells well-known Algonquin ale and lager, and also Black and Tan stout, Hunt Club cream lager, and Bavarian Style Bock beer.

Drive north from Formosa to Highway 4/9, and from there west to Greenock. Greenock Swamp, a huge wetland, straddles Highway 4/9 just west of the village. The swamp supported a thriving lumber industry from 1875 to the early 1900s, when the white pine ran out. Now it attracts naturalists who come to study over 40 species of orchids. The trip continues north from Greenock to Chepstow.

Chepstow warms the heart of any backroad traveller with its quiet millpond (the mill was built in the 1850s and was the nucleus of the community), large church, and the historic King Edward Hotel. The hotel was built in 1871, and the original pine bar is part of a modern-day restaurant and pub. Mr. Pickwick's Parlour offers British pub grub such as a ploughman's lunch and Cornish pasties. The King Edward Restaurant and Tavern sells evening meals and has a Sunday brunch. A quiet old hotel, cheap and filling food, all in a hamlet seemingly forgotten by modern life — what a find!

The landscape north of Chepstow is noticeably more rugged than that near Formosa. There is plenty of subject material here for the photographer: rocky outcrops, steep valleys and tumbling streams, weathered barns, and woods dense with white birch and maple. Turn east on County Road 15 and journey to tiny Pinkerton. Slow down to appreciate the beauty of this mill village, where the houses boast elaborate gingerbreading.

Continue driving east on Road 15 and then north on Road 19, which leads, after an eastward turn, to Chesley, the last town on today's exploration. Local writer and photographer Telford Wegg, whose *Rural Routes* is an excellent travelling companion for today, considers Chesley the "quintessential rural Ontario town." It has street after street of huge Victorian homes, each with a spreading maple on a trim

lawn. Travel along almost any street east from downtown to discover the town park on the banks of the North Saugeen River.

A special treat awaits visitors to Chesley. Drive west along Second Street and follow the river to the millpond. It may appear that the road ends, but at the old wooden mill, turn sharp right and continue across the rickety bridge to the top of the hill. Park the car and turn around to view one of Ontario's loveliest vistas — the ancient McClure Mill, the reflective pond, and the river waters rushing beneath the bridge. The mill has been in the family for over 120 years, and is operated by the fourth generation of McClures.

Today's trip is rich in the comforts of rural country life — trout streams, lowing cattle, wildflowers and village churches — pleasures that will beckon you back for another town-and-country tour of Bruce and Grey Counties.

8 LION'S HEAD
Diamonds in the Rough

The lovely, craggy Niagara Escarpment. Exclusive domain of stalwart campers and hikers, right? Wrong. Those with less than Olympian stamina, take heart, for the Escarpment has many scenic gems that are readily accessible by car. Delay no further, and head out for a tour of the region between Cabot Head and Owen Sound.

Drive north on Highway 6 from Owen Sound. The interior portion of the Bruce Peninsula (the Escarpment proper forms the eastern shoreline) is farm country, where beef production dominates. The pastures are speckled with the yellow, white and red of millions of wildflowers for which the region is famous.

Exit Highway 6 eastward along the road marked for Dyer's Bay, about 80 kilometres  north of Owen Sound. It is hard to believe that such restful countryside still exists in Southern Ontario, but here it is, filled with the melodious song of bobolink and meadowlark. You are as likely to meet a fat porcupine meandering along the side roads as another vehicle. No wonder the Bruce is beloved by cyclists.

At the tiny cottage settlement of Dyer's Bay, turn left (north) and follow signs to Cabot Head Lighthouse. At 9 kilometres, this is not a short jaunt, but press on along this top-notch gravel road wedged between white boulder beaches and looming cliffs. The water of Dyer's Bay will take your breath away with its colour, an intense deep blue at the horizon that fades to pale green at the shore. You have an entire day ahead filled with this brilliantly hued water. Up on the cliffs above is Gillies Lake. It is drained by a small stream that mysteriously disappears underground and reemerges on the cliff face; the stream passes under the roadway about halfway along to Cabot Head. History buffs may want to search just upstream for the remnants of a log flume from the 1880s.

At the end of the road lies Cabot Head Lighthouse, its white silhouette sharply defined against the sky. It stands on a rocky promontory 60 metres above the crashing surf and surveys some of the best scenery on the entire Escarpment. The panorama in both directions is exceptional (especially for those who make the trek up the stairs inside the lighthouse), and photographers will want to leave plenty of time for this attraction. A modest display details the history of the light and of Wingfield Basin, the circular bay visible from the lighthouse. An old shipwreck there is now inhabited by a family of beavers. The nearshore area of flat, rocky barrens is known to scientists as an alvar; a walking trail passes through this alvar to Wingfield Basin.

 Return to the village of Dyer's Bay and retrace your route westbound. Before you reach Highway 6, turn south at Brinkman's Corners. This next rolling stretch of gravel road is known as the Forty Hills (any child will count and let you know that there are actually a few more than 40), and each of these hills is the remains of an ancient coral reef. Stop in at lovely St. Margaret's Chapel (1927) near Cape Chin. This little Anglican church, made of local stone, was built over three years by the congregation. The church with its neatly groomed garden looks just like an English country church. It is always open, so you may take a seat in a pew and enjoy its soothing tranquillity. The sweet perfume of newly cut hay and the sonorous lowing of Holsteins in a pasture close by serve as incense and music for this charming country church. Summertime visitors may wish to take in a Sunday service.

Back to the car and a southbound route. (Explorers are free to try out the numerous roads that lead to the east, such as the ones toward Cape Chin, Smokey Head or White Bluff. Each has its rewards, but one day cannot contain them all.) Eventually you reach the shores of Whippoorwill Bay. White cliffs tower above you, and if you are fortunate enough to be here late in the day, you'll see the rock face shine golden in the setting sun. These famous cliffs were formed from mud and the skeletons of sea creatures under sea water some 400 million years ago. They are a magnificent backdrop for the harbour and village at Lion's Head, which could easily vie for the title of Ontario's prettiest community. There are quiet streets of brick homes, a park decorated with anchors from local shipwrecks, and a sandy swimming beach. Sleek yachts rock rhythmically in the harbour here. The hypnotic spell of Lion's Head makes it hard to pull away, but after an ice cream at the corner store, away you must, southbound along County Road 9.

Follow signs that mark a turn east toward Greig's Caves. This is a privately owned attraction, so there is a modest charge to view the caves. A path runs along the top of those picturesque heights you've been admiring all day, and there are several lookouts. Stairs help hikers make the grand descent to the caves, which are still about 75 metres above Georgian Bay. There are 12 caves in all, connected by a rocky and rugged path. Those with mobility difficulties will want to skip the caves. The caves range in size from a tiny cubbyhole (kids demand to be lifted into this one) to cavernous, arched, house-sized caves. The entire route is covered in lichen and ferns, and water drips continually from trees and cave ceilings. Visitors are interested to learn that Greig's Caves were the setting for the film *Quest for Fire*.

Drive south on County Road 9, which moves away from the water for a few kilometres, only to return to the shore at Colpoys Bay. Many locals consider this deep bay the most attractive section of the entire shoreline. Follow the road around the bay to Spirit Rock Conservation Area, just north of Wiarton. This land belonged to Alexander McNeill, who built a sumptuous 17-room mansion and extensive gardens here in 1881. After a checkered history of care and neglect, the mansion burned to the ground. The stone walls and foundation form a picturesque ruins. There is a lookout over Colpoys Bay as well. Return to the road and the steep hill down into Wiarton.

 Wiarton has several restaurants worth considering for dinner. The Spirit Rock Restaurant, near the conservation area, is recommended by locals. The Barley Bin is at the north end of town. Rough-hewn stone walls and huge beams cast a homespun atmosphere over this former barley mill. For patio dining and a menu that includes Dutch specialties, try the Windmill Restaurant, in the centre of town.

From Wiarton, travel the southern shore of Colpoys Bay, along Frank Street, also County Road 26. There are several parks with viewpoints over the bay and White Cloud Island. If it is more caves that you are after, follow signs to Bruce's Caves Conservation Area. The path to this large cave with an interesting pillar is much easier to walk than the one at Greig's Caves, but the cave itself is less spectacular. There are many species of fern here, including walking fern, slender cliffbrake and polypody. County Road 26 continues along the outer headland as far as Gravelly Bay, where it heads inland. Either continue south to Owen Sound and the end of the trip, or head due west to meet up with Highway 6. This latter route takes you through several somnolent farm villages, including Kemble, Wolseley and Zion.

This day has been a sample of diamonds in the rough — glorious and rugged Niagara Escarpment scenery that is readily accessible to all daytrippers.

9 OWEN SOUND
Sound Advice

Ever had a day when each member of the family wants to do something different — one wants to visit museums, one wants to swim, and one wants to hike? To maintain family harmony for a day, drive to Owen Sound, which offers something for everyone. Discover the gateway to the Bruce Peninsula where Highway 6/10 meets Georgian Bay.

There's plenty of fodder here for the historian. The County of Grey–Owen Sound Museum is located at the intersection of Highway 6/10 and 6th Street East. The main museum building has dioramas, artifacts, photographs and text that describe local goings-on from 1815 to 1930. Don't miss the Native galleries, and the fascinating story of Catharine Sutton, an Ojibwa woman who championed the cause of her people locally and in personal audience with Queen Victoria.

Half a dozen restored buildings illustrate the changes the town has seen — from the pioneer log cabin where tobacco and apples dry over the hearth to a twentieth-century farmhouse rich with the aroma of freshly baked cookies. There is a timber-framed barn, a blacksmith shop, and an old-time automotive garage. Costumed interpreters are experienced hands at answering questions on the herbal dyes used to colour yarn (urine sets the dye really well), and eager to describe the relative ease of the 1920s (only five children to care for, and a central woodburning furnace!).

Downtown Owen Sound has two museums devoted to famous native sons. The Billy Bishop Museum is in the childhood home of the First World War flying ace, Canada's most decorated serviceman. The museum describes the development of modern air warfare — Bishop was central to the process here and in Britain — and the life of a pilot. Those raised in the modern age are amazed to learn that the average life expectancy of a First World War flyer on duty was about one week. The most

40

interesting room contains personal accounts of battles by Bishop and others such as Manfred von Richthofen (the Red Baron). The Bishop Museum is on 3rd Avenue West, at number 948.

Just around the corner on 1st Avenue is the Tom Thompson Memorial Art Gallery, dedicated to one of Canada's most famous artists. Displays chronicle the career of Thompson and contemporaries such as Frank Carmichael and Arthur Lismer. It is interesting to note how many of them came from a photo-engraving and design background. The permanent collection includes paintings and drawings by Thompson and the Group of Seven, and some fine pieces of Native art. The gallery shop has lots of good ideas for the artistically inclined on your gift list.

The last museum on today's agenda is the Marine-Rail Museum, housed in a railway station on the waterfront (1st Avenue West). Travel back to the years when this city was an important railway centre and port. Text and photographs depict the evolution of transportation on the Great Lakes, and there are artifacts from marine foundries and from the Second World War corvette HMCS *Owen Sound*. The railway era is depicted by uniforms, timetables and equipment.

If it's lunchtime, try the 24th Street Roadhouse near the Marine-Rail Museum. It has a patio looking out over the yacht harbour and the immense lake freighters across the bay; the menu ranges from burgers to fajitas, and there's a Sunday buffet.

Families with young children will want to head for popular Story Book Park. Head south on Highway 6/10 about 4 kilometres and turn east on Story Book Park Road. There are several kid-sized rides and attractions, among them a Ferris wheel and roller coaster, water slides and a haunted house, as well as exhibits based on nursery rhymes and stories. A miniature train, minigolf, picnic tables, snack bar and playground round out the park.

Those seeking a swim or a hike can also have their day in Owen Sound. Drive south of town along 2nd Avenue East to beloved Harrison Park. This spacious green space is situated along the Sydenham River. There are many facilities here: swimming pools, paddleboat and canoe rentals, pony rides, horseshoe pits, tennis courts, minigolf, and wildlife displays. The Harrison Park Inn restaurant is open year-round, since the park is open in winter for cross-country and downhill skiing (there is a small hill and rope tow).

Drive farther south of town and you'll find out what happens when the Sydenham River meets the rim of the Niagara Escarpment: 18 metres of white, watery veil decorates rugged stone. This is a terrific spot for a hike, where the legendary Bruce Trail meanders through a verdant, ferny canyon. You can also fish, cycle and cross-country ski here.

Owen Sound is generous to travellers, offering an incredible medley of attractions, from breathtaking scenery to primitive pioneer cabins. It's certainly a town for all seasons, and for all reasons.

County of Grey–Owen Sound Museum
July & August:
Monday–Saturday 9–5
Sunday 1–5
September–June:
Tuesday–Friday 9–5
Saturday & Sunday 1–5
Mid-October–mid-April
only main museum building open
(519) 376-3690

Story Book Park
Late May–October:
Daily 10–6
(519) 376-3069

Billy Bishop Museum
July & August:
Daily 1–4
Mid-May–July &
September–mid-October:
Saturday & Sunday 1–4
(519) 371-0031

Tom Thomson Memorial Art Gallery
July & August:
Daily 10–5
Sunday 12–5
September–June:
Daily 10–5
Sunday 12–5
Wednesday 7–9 PM
(519) 376-1932

Owen Sound Marine–Rail Museum
June–September:
Tuesday–Saturday 10–12 &
1–4:30
Sunday 1–4:30
(519) 271-3333

10 THORNBURY
Fall Fantasy

When September brings a crispness to the air, take a break from the tedium of weekend chores and head outdoors for one last excursion. The Beaver Valley's heady mix of fall fishing, brilliant foliage, and bountiful farm harvests has earned that region a very special place in the hearts of ramblers.

Rise and shine early and head for the shores of bonny Georgian Bay at Meaford. Although Meaford is just outside the Beaver Valley proper, it is usually included in valley tours for its superb apple markets. Apple growing and processing has always been a prosperous element of the Meaford–Thornbury economy because conditions for orchards are perfect: late frosts are rare in the Bighead and Beaver River valleys, Georgian Bay moderates winter storms, and the soils are deep.

Be sure to include at least one farm market on your itinerary. The best known are on Highway 26; they include Gardner's, just west of Meaford, and Almond's, Grandma Lambe's and Goldsmith's, east of town. The air here is richly perfumed with the aroma of freshly baked pies, apple butter and taffy apples, and roadside stands are decorated with pumpkins and gourds. Although the region specializes in McIntosh and Northern Spy apples, there are dozens of other varieties for sale such as Cortland, Greening, Empire and Wellington. Only Gardner's offers a pick-your-own option, which makes for a great family outing. The orchards are gorgeous — succulent red fruit hangs among glossy leaves, all under the deep blue canopy of an Ontario fall sky.

Head into Meaford, a pleasant harbour town where seagulls wheel overhead. If you are coming in from the west side, drive along Susan Street to Scott Clay Products, a small plant that manufactures clay pots, saucers and hot plates. The pots range in size from miniature to gigantic, and the prices are unbeatable. The striking 1907 Opera House surveys downtown Meaford, where there are several craft and gift shops worth looking into, and a good choice of restaurants.

The Meaford Museum, on Bayfield Street near the lakefront, has many artifacts from pioneer days in the area. Most interesting is the ornately carved Speaker's chair from the Canadian Parliament; local MP Dr. Thomas Sproule was Speaker of the House (1911–1915) as well as a senator. Walk along the street to see the snug harbour that shelters Great Lakes sailors and fishermen.

Drive east along Highway 26 toward Thornbury. Long known for its harbour and its trout fishery, Thornbury is also becoming known for shopping and fine dining. Begin at the harbour, where dozens of yachts and powerboats rock against the quay. Next, take a look at the Beaver River. The best vantage point is the trestle bridge, part of the Collingwood-to-Meaford Georgian Trail. (Bike rentals are available at Thornbury Cycle.)

The Beaver River is a top-notch trout stream because of its cold, silt-free waters and gravel bottom. Scores of hipwader-clad folk line the river, and it's fun to watch the action as fortunate anglers scramble along the bank to a shallow spot to land a rainbow trout. These are enormous fish, weighing up to 9 kilograms. The fall migration of rainbows typically takes place in late September or early October. (Call the Ministry of Natural Resources for the best viewing times.)

Walk upstream to where the highway crosses the river. On the north side of the highway is the Thornbury Fish Lock. Most dams are bypassed by means of a fish ladder, however, Thornbury's 7-metre dam is too high for a ladder, and a fish lock, or "elevator" (Ontario's first), was constructed here. Giant trout crowd the base of the lock, and the clear, shallow river is so full of fish that their glistening green-black backs show above the surface. The fish wait patiently, like business people in an office tower, for their turn to enter the elevator. Once inside, the fish travel up to the level of the pond to continue their journey upstream.

Many shops await along Thornbury's main street. Make a special effort to visit a few of them. Savill Brothers Trading Company sells chic casual clothing, and its brightly coloured men's shirts will make your day. The Bluewater Gallery, Textures, Art Glass Studio, and the Three Sisters Gift Shop all supply items with local flavour for home decor. Furbelows, Monica's Boutique, and Tigs have fashionable apparel for women; Cradle & Bear outfits children; and Blow Outs has cheap and plentiful swimsuits for everyone.

Why does a town of 1,500 have so many terrific places to eat? Do some first-hand research yourself, choosing from over a dozen eateries. Four restaurants deserve special attention. Carriages Riverside Inn is located on Highway 26 by the river, on the site of Thornbury's first sawmill, post office and store. This spacious Victorian home was built in 1865, and was purchased in 1912 by William Oldfield, captain of Georgian Bay's first commercial fishing fleet. Carriages offers meals in a British-style restaurant and pub overlooking gardens and the millpond. Favourite dishes include Beaver River trout, rack of lamb in mango-chutney sauce, and chicken Bennington.

Just across the river from Carriages is the Mill Café, specializing in decadent desserts. The deck is as close to the roaring falls as you can get without getting wet. At the southern end of the millpond is the Trillium Restaurant, housed in the 1911 home of a sea captain. Luxuriate on the patio in autumn sunshine and watch golden leaves slowly waft their way from overhead boughs to the serene surface of the pond. Regional food is prepared with European flair. Save room for Grand Marnier cake and crêpe Suzette. For a lighter meal, locals enthusiastically recommend the Picky Palate.

 Travel south from Thornbury on County Road 13. Military enthusiasts head for the village of Clarksburg and the Beaver Valley Military Museum. There are plenty of historic uniforms and equipment, models of aircraft and famous battles, journals, and photos of local regiments. The Beaver River winds its pretty way through

Clarksburg, where one can stop for a relaxing stroll through the riverside park.

Continue southward through apple country. You'll share the highway with flatbed trucks that sway under huge loads of apples. Take the time to enjoy the northward view of orchards and ever-sparkling Georgian Bay. (The view is equally splendid in spring, when each breeze brings a cascade of white petals to the ground.) The road winds along the Beaver River Valley, past hillsides extraordinary with colour in the fall, and with the cliffs of the Niagara Escarpment looming to the east.

Follow the highway to Kimberley, winter haunt of downhill skiers. Just south of Kimberley on the west side of County Road 13 is a pull-off designed for autumn sightseers. The wide-angle view from here of the valley is an uninterrupted swash of orange, russet and red. If you backtrack to County Road 7 and drive a few kilometres north, you'll come to the renowned Epping Overlook and an artist's perspective of the valley. One recommended fall foliage tour is to travel west from Kimberley on County Road 30, from the river to the top of the western valley wall, with a few tight hairpin curves along the way. The view from the rear window of the car is worth the detour. Save some film, though, for the final stop of the day.

Return to Kimberley and drive south on County Road 13. You'll come to the somnolent hamlet of Eugenia. Follow signs to the Eugenia Falls Conservation Area, where all the natural elements of the Beaver Valley can be seen in close-up detail. The mix of deciduous trees and cedar provides maximum colour contrast for photographers. The valley at this point is very narrow and steep, and sinewy tree roots form a Gothic tracery on the jagged cliffs. Eugenia Falls is a fitting place to end a day of great natural beauty.

A description of Beaver Valley reads like a fantasy, the product of a vivid imagination. But it's all real-life splendour that awaits the daytripper every day of the year.

Ministry of Natural Resources
(Owen Sound)
(519) 376-3860

11 COLLINGWOOD
On the Rocks

The Niagara Escarpment is a topographical wonder, a hand-some, rocky ridge that connects Niagara Falls to Tobermory. In the vicinity of Collingwood it forms a grey promontory called Blue Mountain. Come to the mountain for a fun-filled day of history, hiking, fossil-hunting and dining.

Ask any kid, and they'll tell you that mountains are made for climbing up and blitzing down. The folks at Blue Mountain Resorts agree, and have found more uses for a steep incline than you can imagine. The resort is west of Collingwood, reached by way of Highway 26 and Blue Mountain Road (the first stoplight west of town).

 Long known as a skiing centre, Blue Mountain now has an equally active summertime repertoire. One attraction guaranteed to please young and old is the Slide Ride. A ski lift carries riders to the top of the mountain — a trip worth taking for the vista alone. Then, at the top, seat yourself on a mini-bobsled with wheels and rush down almost a kilometre of curving, concrete track at velocities designed to take your breath away. The faint of heart may want to make use of the hand brake that slows the sled to a grandmotherly pace. The fainter-of-heart may ride the chair lift to the bottom. Small children ride the sled with a parent.

There are two more ways to descend the mountain, each allowing you to stay delightfully cool at the same time. The Slipper Dipper water slides (up to 120 metres in length) are fibreglass flumes that curve, crisscross and go through tunnels before descending into the splashdown pool. The Tube Ride consists of one flume, about 3 metres wide, that carries an inner tube and passenger (only those over eight years of age) through falls, pools and rapids. A variety of ticket packages are available: pay as you ride, day-long, a combination of splash and slide rides, and sunset passes for after 3 PM.

To gain an appreciation of the natural and historic aspects of Blue Mountain, head south from the resort along Blue Mountain Road and follow signs to the Scenic Caves and Caverns. The Scenic Caves facility includes a snack bar, gift shop, ice-cream stand and playground. The main draw is a path that leads to the top of the Escarpment (warnings are posted for those with physical conditions that limit exertion) and through a series of caverns and caves.

Fossils embedded in the rock date to a few million years ago, when the cliffs lay underwater. More recently, the Petun and Huron inhabitants used the Escarpment as a defensive fortress, and it is easy to see why. From this 550-metre height, you can survey over 4,000 square kilometres, and apparently signal fires could be seen from Christian Island, Wasaga Beach, Collingwood and Barrie. With brilliant blue Georgian Bay along the horizon and a patchwork of farm fields and Collingwood below, this is one of Ontario's most photogenic locations.

Signs along the pathway point out interesting features. One small cave filled with ice year-round is known as the natural refrigerator. The vegetation is particularly lush in the fern cavern, where Hart's-tongue, maidenhair and walking ferns, a variety of mosses and maidenhair spleenwort hang from the rock face. The expedition ends with challenging Fat Man's Misery. Explorers, in single file, squeeze through a damp cave passage that is only 36 centimetres wide. The contest between man and nature is heightened where the ceiling is quite low and the narrowest point comes at a right-angle turn in the trail! Many visitors opt for the longer but amply sized route outside the cave.

Bobsleds, water flumes and chilly caverns can combine to work up an appetite. Return to the intersection of Blue Mountain Road and Highway 26, the location of the Depot Restaurant. This is Craigleith's original train station, and is decorated with train photographs and other memorabilia. The menu is limited (steaks, ham, parfaits), but only because every item is cooked on the premises by the owner himself. Farther west on Highway 26, at the outdoor patio at Craigleith General Store, you can choose from entrees such as chicken Wellington and rainbow trout. Farther west again is Chez Michel, where you will enjoy attentive service and the exquisite presentation of dishes such as vichyssoise, shrimp flambé in cognac sauce, and raspberry mousse in orange-mango sauce.

Those who still have energy can visit Craigleith Provincial Park, a tiny strip of beach and forest between the highway and Georgian Bay. Craigleith has long been the haunt of paleontologists who seek out trilobite fossils from the 445-million-year-old shale along the shore. A perfect combination of wind and surf makes Craigleith a destination for windsurfers and kayakers. The colourful sails and craft make for another good photo opportunity.

There's more than one way to enjoy a mountain, and Blue Mountain offers enough opportunities for outdoor fun to last an entire season.

Blue Mountain Resorts
Great Slide Ride:
Mid-May–mid-June &
mid-September–mid-October:
Weekends only 10–5
Mid-June–mid-September:
Daily, varying hours
Waterpark:
Mid-June–early September:
Daily 9:30–7
(705) 445-0231

Scenic Caves and Caverns
Late May–mid-October:
Daily, dawn to dusk
(705) 446-2828

12 COLLINGWOOD
First Port of Call

Port cities are enchanting places. They carry an air of excitement; it seems that somebody is always going somewhere — whether aboard a freighter bearing a foreign flag, or on a small sailcraft for a holiday tour. And then there's the infinite wide blue horizon for hours of contemplation, and fresh marine breezes to relish. No port in Ontario exemplifies this charm as well as Collingwood.

Start out at the Collingwood Museum, located near the harbour on St. Paul Street in a Northern Railway Line train station that dates to the mid-1800s. The museum traces local history from the time of the Petun to the days of the Jesuit missionaries to Collingwood's years as an important shipyard and port.

The museum shines when it portrays life in a shipbuilding town. W. Watts & Sons were the makers of agile and speedy boats, the winners of numerous yachting trophies, and won Collingwood a continent-wide reputation. Examine their tools of the trade — sailmaker's palms, spoke shears, splicing fids, marlin spikes. Lovely historic photographs, models, diagrams and journals tell the story of Collingwood as the Chicago of the north, a terminus of railway and water transport, and a town flourishing with marine businesses. An intriguing video allows visitors to join the thousands who gathered to watch the 1979 launch of the *Algoport*, a 200-metre, steel-hulled freighter built in Collingwood.

After a museum visit, drive west along the lakeshore. Turn north on Birch Street to visit White's Fisheries for some Georgian Bay splake, whitefish, perch and chub. Continue along Birch to Harbourview Park for a look at Collingwood's gargantuan grain elevators and sailing harbour. From Harbourview Park, you can head out on the Georgian Trail, a beautiful 32-kilometre bicycle and walking trail that follows the route of an abandoned railbed from Collingwood to Thornbury and Meaford.

Collingwood is famous for its harbour, as well as for Blue Mountain pottery made from the marl clay of the Niagara Escarpment. Souvenir hunters should continue west along Highway 26 to its right-angle turn north. Blue Mountain Pottery is in a mall just north of this turn. The store there carries a host of pottery figurines — animals and people — with the trademark glossy blue or green glaze. During working hours visitors can watch the production process. Across the street from the pottery shop is Little Ed's Ski Shop, where you can rent kids' and adults' bikes; the Georgian Trail is accessible from Ed's parking lot.

Return to the centre of town and turn south on Pine Street. Look for the nautical decorations on the streetlamps. Between First and Third, Pine Street is a good wander, with several cafés and clothing stores. The strip is anchored at each end with a must-see. At the north end is Clerkson's, in a historic home with an outstanding perennial garden. There's so much neat stuff to look at in Clerkson's, embracing all the latest trends in home decoration: stick furniture, sunflower-motif kitchenware, Southwestern blankets and baskets, Ontario antiques (painted and au naturel), and other distinctive folk art. Bet you can't leave empty-handed.

At the south end of the Pine Street shopping area is Christopher's, a restaurant housed in a remarkable pink stone mansion built in 1901 for a doctor's family. Furnished in period decor, the house has garments that belonged to the original lady of the house displayed along the stairway; the walls are adorned with family photographs. Christopher's serves lunch, dinner and afternoon tea daily. The seasonal menus feature local products; springtime dinners bring asparagus and strawberries, and fall dinners highlight wild game and apple dishes. Edible flower garnishes come from Christopher's own garden.

While on Pine Street, take the opportunity to wander west along Third Avenue. During the glory days of Great Lakes shipping, great wealth was generated in Collingwood, as evidenced by several blocks of grand mansions. A walking-tour brochure is available from local merchants. The house at 144 Pine and other neighbouring homes have "flower pot" designs, a feature unique to Collingwood mansions, decorating their gables. Most notable are a pair of houses on the corner of Third and Oak Streets. Constructed in the 1890s for a biscuit-manufacturing family, the Telfers, the houses reflect the Victorian love of architectural flourishes — towers, gables and ornate decoration.

 Collingwood has another historic home turned restaurant, Grant's Spike and Spoon. Drive to the main street, and turn south to 637 Hurontario. On land originally owned by Sir Sandford Fleming this spacious brick home was built in 1905 for the Hodgsons, a circus family. The maitre d' provides an interesting history of the house and some of the notables who have been guests here. Dine on ample servings of international foods such as marinated calamari, angel-hair noodles with vegetables in tomato cream, and tortilla spring rolls.

Those who seek a variety-filled day won't want to delay a visit to Collingwood. This harbour town has so much going for it, you'll want to make it your first port of call.

Collingwood Museum
Mid-June–September:
Saturday 10–5
Sunday 12–4
September–Mid-June:
Wednesday–Saturday 12–5
(705) 445-4811

Little Ed's Ski Shop
(705) 444-5488

13 CREEMORE
Nooks and Crannies

A re you one of those people who loves to head off in search of adventure, exploring Ontario's nooks and crannies for nature walks and tiny villages far from throngs of ordinary tourists? Look no further than the byways of Simcoe County for just such a day.

Simcoe County is bordered on the west by the Niagara Escarpment, where its cliffs rise to over 500 metres above sea level near Singhampton. Devil's Glen Provincial Park (on Highway 24 just east of Singhampton), perched on the rim of the Escarpment, is a convenient starting point for today's trip. Although government cutbacks mean that Devil's Glen is not staffed, the public is welcome to walk into the park. A highlight is the lookout over the Mad River Valley. You are at eye-level with the soaring hawks and turkey vultures that take advantage of the wind currents funnelled through the valley. Display boards describe how the valley was formed by glacial meltwater.

 Head for the 2.5-kilometre trail, an extension of the Bruce Trail. (Those who find steep pathways and stairs difficult may want to avoid the trail's 75-metre descent.) The upper slopes are covered with fragrant white cedars, while nearer the river there are dense clumps of hawthorn, chokecherry and dogwood. Wildflowers and their attendant butterflies are present in abundance. Keep an eye out for 23 species of fern, especially the rare Hart's-tongue and smooth cliffbrake ferns. The Mad River is well named, since its shallow waters seem in a noisy rush to reach their destination, making this location an idyllic menage of ferns, flowers and water song.

After the climb back up the Escarpment, drive east on Highway 24 and then south on County Road 62 toward Glen Huron, a hamlet that has survived on the success of the water-powered Hamilton Brothers Sawmill since 1874. Turn west at Sideroad 12/13. A couple of kilometres along, there is a sign indicating

Bruce Trail parking on the north side of the road.

The trail follows a road allowance between farm fields and then ascends the towering grey Escarpment. The trail leads to the very edge of the cliff where the world is laid out at your feet. A patchwork of gold, emerald and bronze stretches to the horizon; red barns and church steeples mark each hilltop; the scent of hay and the song of meadowlarks are carried on the breeze.

When you've filled your soul with peace, come down from the mountaintop to rejoin humanity. Drive east on Sideroad 12/13, south on County Road 62 and then east again, to Creemore. Creemore is one of those villages that makes an Ontarian sigh with pride: blocks of century-old, redbrick homes with front verandahs, tree-arched streets, and an interesting mix of shops and restaurants.

The Creemore Clock Company sells clocks, some over 200 years old. There are wall clocks deeply carved with hunting scenes, grandfather clocks with brass faces, and elegant mantel clocks. The shop uses myriad leftover clockworks to fashion truly unique jewellery — earrings, necklaces, brooches — designed to delight even the most jaundiced shopper. Another real find is Ragged Rats Clothing Company. Each item of children's wear, from melton bomber-jackets to yachting suits, is designed and handmade by the youthful owner. The Creemore Curiosity Shop has a wonderful collection of books, ranging from literature to local travel guides to cookbooks. There are too many craft and antique shops in and around Creemore to mention each individually, but merchants are happy to provide a local map and listing.

Creemore's primary claim to fame is the Creemore Springs Brewery, located right on the main street. Aficionados of independent breweries may tour the plant that produces premium-quality brews from natural ingredients and buy Creemore Springs clothing and mugs as well as beer. Just around the corner is Creemore's other claim to fame, its jail, billed as the smallest in the province at about 5 metres by 6 metres.

The first resident of the jail was a runaway black cow; later inhabitants included the indigent and drunks.

There are several eateries in Creemore. The well-known Sovereign Restaurant, located in an 1890 hotel, serves goulash and platters piled high with schnitzel. Dessert is equally satisfying and may include palacsinta (crêpes with apricot and walnut filling), eight-layered bishop's torte or rum cake. The Sovereign is open for dinner year-round, and during summer weekends extends its hours to include lunch. The menu at the Old Mill House, located on the main street, includes steak, stir-fries and chicken, European pastries and cheesecake.

 No matter what direction is home, take the time to explore the country side roads west of Creemore. Take Caroline Street west to the 5th Line southbound, and then any of the westbound roads from there. Rediscover a rural Ontario that has just about vanished. Tidy farms are widely spaced along gravel roads, and every hill provides a view that stretches all the way to Georgian Bay.

An enjoyable day spent in Ontario's nooks and crannies is guaranteed to all who travel the backroads of western Simcoe County.

Creemore Jail
May–October:
Daily 10–6

14 WASAGA BEACH
Life's a Beach

One result of travel is often the dispelling of stereotypes, and there's no better example of this than a day spent at Wasaga Beach. Long identified as the haunt of the noisy sun-and-surf crowd, Wasaga has worked hard to polish its image, and is now a rewarding destination for everyone.

Daytrippers who haven't visited Wasaga Beach for some time will be delighted to discover the Nancy Island Historic Site on Mosley Street near Beach 2. Follow signs to the site, where the theatre looks like a schooner's billowing sails. Nancy Island is devoted to Wasaga Beach in its early days, when it was a British naval shipyard called Schooner Town.

The main exhibit area is in a building that shelters the remains of the H.M.S. *Nancy*. The *Nancy* was a strong and fleet schooner, built in 1789, that measured about 25 metres in length, 6.5 metres in width, and had a capacity of 350 barrels. She was active in the fur trade until commandeered to serve the British during the War of 1812. After the disastrous Battle of Lake Erie, the *Nancy* was the sole British ship on the Upper Lakes, and supplied strategically significant Fort Mackinac near Sault Ste. Marie. Although the ship was well hidden several kilometres up the Nottawasaga River, the Americans planned an attack. The badly outnumbered British Navy burned the *Nancy* to prevent her capture.

It seems as if the ship was not ready to retire from Canadian history, however, as its hull formed the basis of a sand bar in the river; that sand bar collected silt over 114 years and eventually turned into Nancy Island. The hull, keel and ribs of the ship are now carefully preserved in the island museum. The same building contains several excellent displays of text, uniforms, maps and artifacts on the War of 1812, shipbuilding (ships were built from models, not blueprints), and life in the

British navy (flogging, signal flags, and knot-tying). The most unusual display provides the naval origins of commonly used expressions such as "son of a gun," "toe the line," "not enough room to swing a cat" and "groggy." There are ropes available for visitors to try their hand at imitating the marine knots, splices and "fancy work" on display.

The museum theatre also has additional displays, and movies play several times daily. Kids love to climb the replica Great Lakes lighthouse, and just can't resist ringing the huge ship's bell. Museum staff run an interpretive program on Native games and legends, campfire songs and stories (spooks 'n' sparks), and the life of a voyageur.

 How ironic that the very factors that led to the abandonment of Schooner Town — high winds, shifting sand bars and a long, unprotected shore — are the very conditions that made Wasaga Beach a popular holiday town. The winds are perfect for windsurfing, the sand bars mean that even youngsters can wade a long way out, and the beach, part of the longest freshwater beach in the world, has 14 kilometres of fine white sand.

While much of the shoreline is privately owned, there is plenty of space for everyone at Wasaga Provincial Park's six beach areas. (Beach 1 is farthest east and Beach 6 farthest west.) Each beach has its own picnicking sites, bike paths, parking lot, change rooms and playgrounds. The eastern beaches tend to be busier, perhaps because they are conveniently located near a hub of fast-food restaurants and beachwear stores. Beach 1 is the site of the Van Vlack Display Court, which details the history of the local logging industry; this beach also has a boat launch and fishing platforms. Windsurfers are advised to head a little north of Beach 1 for winds that hit the shore at a good angle for getting out on the waves, and where there are fewer swimmers to avoid. There are all sorts of ways to enjoy a beach, and at Wasaga you'll see every one of them: jet skis, inner tubes and air mattresses, football, volleyball and just plain playing catch.

Even if you are not a sun bunny, Wasaga Beach has a place for you. Follow signs along River Road West (Highway 92) to the Blueberry Plains Trail. Popular during the winter for cross-country skiing, this nature area, deserted during the summer, can be a welcome respite from the kinetic activity at the beach. There are actually several trails, but the most recommended is the Blueberry Plains, a pleasant stroll or bike of about 3 kilometres through deciduous forest.

Whether you are a swimmer, a wader or a simple seeker of summer relaxation, Wasaga Beach is the place to be.

Wasaga Beach Provincial Park
Open daily, year-round

Nancy Island Historic Site
Mid-May–mid-June:
Saturday & Sunday 10–6
Mid-June–September:
Daily 10–6
(705) 429-2516

15 AWENDA PROVINCIAL PARK
A Friend for Life

A wenda Provincial Park, located at the northern tip of Simcoe County, is one of the lesser-known members of our lovely provincial park system. Its 2,500 hectares of woodlands, beaches and historic sites await your discovery. Drive to Penetanguishene by way of Highway 93 or Highway 12, and then follow signs to Awenda.

The log-cabin trail centre, run by the volunteers of Friends of Awenda, is the place to find out about Awenda's trails and interpretive programs.

Visitors usually head for Awenda's 21 kilometres of hiking trails (or, in winter, 32 kilometres of groomed ski-trails). Most of the trails are wide and suitable for bicycles as well as feet. No matter which route you select, you'll quickly notice Awenda's unique terrain. Unlike much of Georgian Bay's shoreline, which is exposed bedrock, Awenda is covered by a thick layer of glacial debris that formed into cobble beaches, shoreline dunes, and the 32-metre Nipissing Bluff. The original white pine and hemlock forest was removed during the late 1800s by ship-builders and farmers. The forest of today is young and verdant, comprising aspen, maple, birch and oak. Awenda also has an interesting, and very mixed, human history. This was the territory of at least four different Native societies, as well as logging and farming settlements. The park has 17 archaeological sites, and you can take one of several guided hikes to learn more about its history.

Awenda has six hiking trails: Brûlé, Wendat, Beach, Bluff, Dunes and Beaver Pond. Brûlé is an easy 2-kilometre walk through campgrounds and forest. The self-guiding brochure for 5-kilometre-long Wendat (Wendat, also spelled Ouendat, is what the Huron called themselves) explains the trail's 12 interpretive stops.

This is a good trail to take if you want to explore glacial
shoreline as well as the wetland and old-growth forest
around Second Lake. The 2-kilometre Beach Trail is the
best way to access each of Awenda's four beaches. The trail is connected to Bluff Trail by way of 155 steps on the face of Nipissing
Bluff. Springs at the base of the bluff mean that the forest at the
bottom of the slope is damp; cedar, hemlock and birch grow here,
in sharp contrast to the dry uplands on top of the bluff.

The Bluff Trail is the longest walk, at 12 kilometres, and is
named for the Nipissing Bluff along which it runs. The promontory
is actually a raised beach marking the shoreline of glacial Lake
Nipissing, created about 8,000 years ago. The Dunes Trail is a short
walk to a 76-metre, top-of-the-world lookout over sand dunes,
Christian Island and Methodist Point. The foundations of an abandoned farmstead are visible from the trail, and visitors are asked
not to disturb this site or the fragile dunes. Beaver Pond Trail is a
wheelchair-accessible boardwalk through marshland, and its lookout platform, washrooms and picnic site are all barrier-free.

Awenda's trails are recommended for bird-watchers.
The forest is inhabited by some species usually found farther north, such as the Swainson's warbler, as well as
southern cerulean warblers and yellow-throated vireos.
Most recently, excitement was created by the confirmation of a
pair of nesting hooded warblers, which are uncommon in Ontario.
Those with a botanical interest arrive in the spring to see orchids
and trilliums (white, red and painted) and return in fall for the
brilliant foliage.

Awenda is not only forest and lookouts over the bay. Second
Lake is a kettle lake, formed when a giant chunk of glacial ice
was buried by the retreating glaciers. This underground ice-block
melted slowly, and its basin formed the lake. Second Lake is
much loved by canoeists, who come to watch wetland wildlife in
 a motorboat-free locale. Kids love to ply the waters
for panfish and bass.

Powerboaters head for the open waters of Georgian Bay.
Awenda includes Giant's Tomb Island; according to Native legend,

Ait is the resting place of the spirit Kitchikewana. Boaters may take advantage of the island's 480 hectares for picnicking, hiking, swimming and fishing. The water between the main park and Giant's Tomb is popular with those who fish for pike and pickerel.

Awenda park naturalists guide owl prowls, spirit walks, herptile walks, and kids' programs of crafts, legends and games. Live animals are often special guests at these events.

After working up a sweat on the trails, head for the water to cool off. Although Georgian Bay has a reputation for cool water, the shallow beaches at Awenda warm up to a pleasant temperature. Those temperatures, the natural "shelves" of shallow water formed by wave action, the unusual boulders strewn in the shallows, and the complete lack of crowds, all combine to make Awenda a favourite with families. This is especially true of the beaches at Methodist Point, where Awenda juts into Georgian Bay.

Awenda is translated from the Huron as, "Trust me, I am your friend." Awenda's many fans are confident that visitors can indeed trust the park for a variety-filled excursion.

Awenda Provincial Park
Park open year-round
Most services closed in winter
(705) 549-2231

16 PENETANGUISHENE
Hoist Those Sails, Mates

Visitors to Penetanguishene's Discovery Harbour had better come prepared to join in the work of a shipshape naval depot. Swab the deck! Hoist the sails! Pull the oars! The orders and salt-dog insults are offered by good-natured staff in full costume who help — or cajole — visitors into everyday chores at this working frontier settlement.

The British chose this site as a supply depot because of its protected and easily defended harbour. By 1820, the base had 20 vessels, 30 build- ings, and supported about 70 sailors, civilians and their families. The village of today comprises several carefully constructed and very believable replicas of buildings typical of the period.

The first sight of Discovery Harbour draws a gasp from all who come here. It seems a scene straight out of history: three beautiful tall ships are moored at a wharf that is encircled by bright rose and blue warehouses. Bayfield's Charthouse is the place to join an interpretive tour and to sign up for a cruise on either H.M. *Schooner Tecumseth* or H.M. *Schooner Bee*. (Visitors may want to phone in advance, as this highly recommended activity is very popular.)

One of the first calls on land is to Dr. Todd's house, where young and old alike squirm as they learn about bloodletting and amputations without anesthetics. Todd's front porch makes a prime post for a survey of the active harbour area. Listen to the whirring sawmills as timbers are squared, the clang of hammer on anvil at the smithy, the jangle of horse brasses, and the ring of a ship's bell.

 The tour moves on through the sailor's barracks, where up to 30 men and boys, some as young as ten, would sleep, fight, play games, and partake of salted meat and scurvy-preventing limes. Children are invited to try their hand at swinging into the suspended hammocks, a task easier said than done. All are surprised to learn that a hammock was a very personal item, and that burial at sea meant being sewn into your hammock and tossed overboard.

 One of the most interesting stops is the home of cartographer Lieutenant Bayfield, who resided here with his staff for two years while he mapped the Great Lakes. His work was in official use until the 1960s, and is still considered a model of accuracy. Furnishings include early surveyor's instruments and maps, and oilskin clothing that you can try on.

Nearby are the rather cramped quarters of commanding officer Captain Roberts, who lived here with his young wife and sister in-law. These women, along with the doctor's wife, lived in a community with few of their own sex, and because the language and behaviour of the sailors would be less than civil, their lives would have taken place entirely indoors, or under escort. Roberts found the living conditions here beneath his station: the floorboards of the house were under water during wet weather, wind entered at every crack and cranny, and he lacked a study for his paperwork.

When the British Navy left the base in the 1830s, the army moved in. The last home of the day, and the only original building, is the army officers' quarters. It was built of local limestone and housed a servant and two or three unmarried officers. The furnishings depict the sporting life of the well-to-do. There are snowshoes and hunting gear in the bedrooms, and the dining room is elegantly appointed, complete with lead wine-box and portraits of Victoria and Albert.

The tour ends with a horse-drawn carriage ride back to Bayfield's Charthouse. From there, wander down to the harbour, the real heart of the community. Discovery Harbour's most illustrious residents are the *Tecumseth*, a 137-metre supply ship from the War of 1812; and the 24-metre *Bee*, a transport schooner stationed here from 1817 to the 1830s. Admiralty plans and rigging inventory were carefully followed to make these ships look just like the originals. Three-hour sails are offered morning and afternoon, as well as at sunset, and the crews — in navy felt jackets, straw hats and neckerchiefs — enlist passengers to hoist the sails (no mean feat considering the *Tecumseth* has over 500 square metres of canvas) and to sweep (row) the ship to the dock. The sails are suitable for kids over ten, adults and active seniors.

Fresh sea breezes quicken any appetite, so after a sail, head to Captain Roberts Table for seafood chowder, roast beef and syllabub (the latter adapted from original recipes). Evenings, enjoy comedies and musicals at the King's Landing Warehouse, or on Wednesdays take in a conducted lantern tour. Summer events include fiddle orchestra concerts, art shows, and children's craft clubs, and there are special programs at Hallowe'en and Christmas.

Discovery Harbour is a sure-fire winner, a combination of fresh-air cruises, entertainment, and hands-on history lesson.

Discovery Harbour
Mid-May–mid-October:
Daily 10–5
Sails
July & August:
Tuesday, Thursday & Saturday 5:15 PM
Monday, Wednesday, Friday & Sunday 10 & 2
Fall colour sails in September
(705) 549-8064

17 PARRY SOUND
30,000 Reasons to Tarry in Parry

B onny Parry Sound is the envy of cottage country, for while it abounds in tourist attractions — 30,000 Island boat cruises, harbour, shops, restaurants and a museum — it has not sold its rugged, northern soul for the sake of a dollar, and remains a lovely town to live in.

 A Parry Sound day properly starts with an overview — with the emphasis on the over — from the fire tower. From Highway 69, follow signs to the West Parry Sound District Museum, which shares grounds with the tower. Climb the tower for a complete perspective of the harbour, the CP trestle bridge, and Parry Island. Descend the tower to enter one of the province's best regional museums, housed in an 1893 fire station.

Polished exhibits of text, artifacts and photographs focus on economic activities such as lumbering, farming, shipbuilding and tourism. Each section puts a human face on history. There is a fascinating taped interview with a lumberjack, describing his difficult and dangerous life working in the bush for 57 years. There's plenty of information on lumber baron J.R. Booth, whose Ottawa, Arnprior & Parry Sound Railway made Parry Sound a major lumber and grain port.

Surprisingly, farming was once an important occupation in this land of rock and swamp, oats being a crucial commodity in a lumber town powered by horses. Place names such as Poverty Bay, Distress River and Hungry Lake are all that remain of the attempts to gather grain from bedrock. The museum does a good job of retelling the grim story of whole farm communities pulling up stakes for the more fertile prairies.

It's time to head downhill to the harbour and the *Island Queen*; a voyage on this huge, 40-metre-long, 525-tonne vessel should be the focal point of a day spent in Parry Sound. Three-hour narrated cruises embark twice daily for the world's largest freshwater archipelago, the 30,000 Islands. The *Island Queen* trip is recommended for comfort (there are hundreds of seats to choose from) and for the captain's narration, which is the best among cottage country cruises.

The scenery of the 30,000 Islands never disappoints. Wind-twisted pine and spruce cling to pink granite that plunges into the dark water from high cliffs; islands are close at hand and fill the middle distance; at the western horizon, blue water reaches out to meet the curve in the Earth's surface. Cottaging has been popular here for almost a century, but unlike in other parts of the province, where "cottage" means an imposing glass-and-cedar house, these modest island retreats tend to be simple log or frame cabins still in the age of oil lamps and propane appliances.

The captain's narration provides intriguing details on many sites and stories: composer Irving Berlin's summer haunt; Parry Island, home to the Wasauksing First Nation and site of ghost town Depot Harbour; the *Waubuno*, a steamship that sank in 1879; the island retreat of the Eaton family; and Amanda Island, a luxurious estate willed by millionaire Charlie Band to his nurse, Amanda.

Before there were cottages and boats on Georgian Bay, there was wildlife. The *Island Queen* takes in two locales popular with wildlife watchers. The first is Gull Island, a small bird sanctuary where dozens of gulls, terns, great blue heron and cormorants nest, dry out and squawk a warning at passers-by. The second is an osprey nest high atop a specially constructed platform. The *Island Queen*'s upper deck provides a perfect vantage point for observing the ever-vigilant birds up close.

If it is time for a meal when you return to harbour, there's the Bay Street Café across the street from the dock for burgers, local pickerel, and creative pizzas. Or walk up to the main street of town and two remarkable bakeries. At Der Brot Korb on Seguin Street, you'll find a celebration of breads, with round, golden San Francisco bread, long baguettes, and speckled sunflower rye and muesli loaves. Country Gourmet on James Street, just around the corner, is the place to put together a gourmet picnic hamper from uncommon items such as head cheese and cucumber salad, mustard seed salami, and assorted cheeses, from gorgonzola to asiago. The luscious desserts include lemon yogurt torte, and nougat, marzipan and chocolate squares. Both locations are good for eating in or takeout.

At the corner of James and Seguin are four fine shops housed under one handsome roof: Parry Sound Books, with an excellent selection of fiction, children's and Northern books; Whiskey Jack, a craft gallery that specializes in stained-glass work; and Georgian Bay Summer Collection and Florence's Finery Shoppe, for classic casual clothing.

Delectable food, shopping, a good museum and 30,000 islands are plenty of reasons to tarry in Parry year after year.

West Parry Sound Museum
June–October:
Daily 10–4
November–May:
Tuesday & Wednesday 1–4
(705) 746-5365

The Island Queen
June–mid-October:
2 PM
July & August
10 & 2
(705) 746-2311

18 MIDLAND
Huronia Heritage

The people of northern Huronia — the peninsula that stretches toward the islands of Georgian Bay and includes the communities of Midland and Penetanguishene — are intensely proud of their region's history. That pride is well founded, and a day spent touring Midland will open your eyes to the fact that some of Ontario's earliest settlements, both Native and European, were established here.

To begin at the beginning, visit the Huron Indian Village and Huronia Museum; these two attractions are side by side in centrally located Little Lake Park. The main entrance to the park is off King Street, the main street of town. Tour the palisaded village that recreates the Huron way of life of a thousand years ago. You'll see several longhouses, complete with cooking fires, sleeping platforms, hanging pelts, and baskets of smoked fish, dried corn and tobacco. The village also includes a medicine man's lodge, a wigwam for visiting tribes, a sweat bath and a lookout tower. A variety of implements are displayed, from hide scrapers to moss racks (cradles), and lacrosse sticks to canoes.

After the village, enter the Huronia Museum. Be sure to see the exquisite grass, willow and ash baskets elaborately decorated with porcupine quills in the Native arts collection. Much of the museum is taken up with household items: toys, looms, clocks, Victorian clothing, housewares, shipping records and lighting fixtures. Visitors will be impressed with the extensive display of Canadian paper money from the days when each bank issued its own currency. The gallery displays works by notables William J. Wood, Frank Johnston and A.Y. Jackson. The gift shop's collection of books on Native Canadian stories and culture is outstanding.

Next on the agenda is Midland's premier attraction, Sainte-Marie among the Hurons. Exit Little Lake Park onto King Street south and turn left at Heritage Drive (Highway 12). The location of Sainte-Marie is well-marked and is just over the Wye River.

Sainte-Marie, one of Parks Canada's many exceptional facilities, is an accurate reconstruction of the seventeenth-century Jesuit mission that was Ontario's first European community. An engaging film describes life in the fortified village, which served as a refuge for itinerant missionaries. The film presents a story of cultural tension, as the relationship between the French and the local Wendat people led to epidemics, famine, intertribal warfare and the ultimate disappearance of Wendat society. The film is a wonderful vehicle for transporting visitors back in time 350 years: the screen rolls up and there you are, at the doorway to a village of the mid-1600s.

 Staff in period costume reenact daily routines, playing the parts of the "black robes" and the Native Christian converts. These minidramas occur throughout the village, in the smithy and barns, at the long tables in the dining room, and near the birchbark cross in the Church of St. Joseph. Guests are invited to bake cornbread, weave baskets, tend fires and chop firewood. Younger visitors are captivated as history comes alive before their eyes.

Sainte-Marie's museum uses audiovisual displays, maps and dioramas to detail the experiences of the early settlers, from social unrest in Europe in the sixteenth and seventeenth centuries to life on the lonely frontier.

Summer afternoon canoe trips turn a day at Sainte-Marie into pure adventure. These 90-minute excursions, in 7-metre canoes like those used by the missionaries, transport visitors through the marsh for an explorer's view of Sainte-Marie. Candlelight tours take place on summer evenings, and there are daily and weekly kids' summer camps. The park has a restaurant — the best bet for lunch today — and a gift shop.

Across Highway 12 from Sainte-Marie, and reached by car or by walking along a footpath under the bridge, is famous Martyrs' Shrine (1926). The massive, twin-spired church dominates the landscape for kilometres around, its silvery stone glinting in the sunlight. The twentieth-century shrine was built in memory of the Jesuits who laboured at Sainte-Marie. Eight of these men were killed by Iroquois; Brébeuf and Lalemant are buried at Sainte-Marie. Six of the original brothers were canonized, the first men on the continent to be thus recognized. Pilgrims come from around the world to attend mass, use the picnic grounds, explore the church (there is a self-guiding brochure available), and see the site of Pope John Paul II's visit. There is a small cafeteria and gift shop.

You've walked through more than a thousand years of Ontario's history — all in a day's trip to Huronia.

Huronia Museum and Huron Indian Village
January–April:
Monday–Saturday 9–5
Sunday 12–5
May–August:
Monday–Saturday 9–5
Sunday 10–5
September–December:
Monday–Saturday 9–5
Sunday 10–5
(705) 526-2844

Sainte-Marie among the Hurons
Mid-May–mid-October:
Daily 10–5
(705) 526-7838

Martyrs' Shrine
Mid-May–September:
Daily mass at 9, 10:30, 12 & 7:30
Devotions 3 PM
Grounds and church 9–9
(705) 526-3788

19 WYEBRIDGE
Bridge on the River Wye

Wyebridge is a placid little village that many travellers might overlook in their rush along Highway 93 to reach Georgian Bay. But short stopovers at Wyebridge and the Wye Marsh Wildlife Centre make a perfect antidote to city hustle and bustle. They are gateways to a relaxed, cottage frame of mind.

 One reason Wyebridge is so pleasant is that its shops are located in century-old houses, and thus don't detract from the village street scene. Wyebridge Country is the largest of the stores in town, and the antique lawn-bowling table (for storing balls and other paraphernalia) at the entrance is one sign that this store sells some unique items. There are several rooms of china, linens, picnic baskets, candles and glassware — whatever is needed for fashionable entertaining. For home decor with the outdoors look, there are hammocks, fishing creels, picnic baskets and dried flowers. Step outside the back door to appreciate the outstanding garden.

Wyebridge Whimsies is an antique shop crammed to the rafters with china, glassware, lamps, historic prints and paintings. There are plenty of antique tables, china cabinets and dressers to hold all these treasures. Expert advice and a search service are available to those tracking down a special antique or contemporary piece of tableware. Grass Roots stocks an eclectic mix of gourmet foods, luxurious lingerie, casual clothing, jewellery and candles. Christine's Gift Boutique offers a wide assortment of items for home accents: quilts, pottery, lace, and designer dolls for young and old.

Lunchtime is the time to visit Meg's on the Wye, the café in the riverside board-and-batten building that dates to the 1860s. Soup, salad and sandwiches are served up with imagination: endive, red cabbage, mandarin oranges and walnuts make a colourful salad, and a simple sundae is a two-storey affair of brownies, ice cream, sauce and whipped cream. Upstairs from Meg's, the Clockwork Mouse Toy Company has everything you could want for a well-stocked nursery, from musical mobiles to a complete selection of Pooh and Beatrix Potter collectibles.

Wyebridge is only the beginning of a slow-track trip to the cottage. The Wye River leads to Georgian Bay, and at the river mouth is the wonderful, watery world of the Wye Marsh Wildlife Centre. (Take Highway 93 to Highway 12 and then follow signs to the centre.) Over a decade ago, government funding for the centre ceased, but a group of determined and energetic supporters rallied, and Wye Marsh is now a private, non-profit organization.

Summertime interpretive programs feature a live birds-of-prey exhibition, and theatre presentations on marsh inhabitants such as dragonflies, bees and reptiles. Sunday programs are devoted to the elegant trumpeter swan, and explain the conservation work of Wye Marsh staff. Trumpeter swans, graceful white birds that were common in this region two centuries ago, came close to extinction due to overhunting and habitat reduction. The centre has two breeding pairs of swans, and the cygnets raised each year in their own special pond are released into the wild. Unfortunately, many young swans have died from lead poisoning from the lead shot lying on the bottom of the marsh. Because of this problem, an education program has been created with the aim of convincing hunters to use alternative shot.

The highlight of the summer programs is the canoe excursion. These guided tours of the marsh leave three times daily; they take about 45 minutes and are an excellent way to glimpse muskrat, turtles and wildflowers, and a buzzing, squeaking, singing host of birds and insects. Kids over the age of six can dig into the work of paddling with gusto as they point out the animals they've learned to identify. Phone the visitor centre to reserve a place on the tours.

Wye Marsh has two annual events, the Wye Marsh Festival in September, and the Sweetwater Harvest when the maple sap runs in March. Bird-watchers find spring and fall most rewarding at Wye Marsh, since it is an important migration rest-stop for waterfowl. A bird checklist of 222 species is available in the nature centre; from there you will want to head for the blinds and lookouts over the marsh and open water to observe the ducks, herons, rails, gulls and terns. The walking trails through woodland and abandoned farmland are recommended diversions for when bitter winds whip over the marsh, chilling face and hands. Another good retreat is the nature centre, with its displays on marsh ecology and trumpeter swans, and a gift shop with posters, books and toys.

The action at Wye Marsh continues all winter long on 20 kilometres of groomed and track-set ski trails. The trails lead to lookouts over the entire Wye Valley, where the snow glistens bright against the tall conifers. Rentals and light refreshments are available and there are outdoor campfire sites. Guided wildlife excursions, moonlight skiing and school-holiday ski camps are part of the winter interpretive programs. Youngsters delight at feeding Wye Marsh's tame chickadees, and the nature centre obliges by providing bird seed (cleverly packed in old film tubes) free of charge.

Quaint Wyebridge and serene Wye Marsh are so enjoyable that you may not make it to the cottage at all.

Wye Marsh Wildlife Centre
Mid-May–September:
Daily 10–6
September–mid-May:
Daily 10–4
(705) 526-7809

20 BEAUSOLEIL ISLAND
What's in a Name?

Daytrippers need to get it right, right from the start. The name of this fascinating island may be Beausoleil on the maps, but in the minds of locals, the name is Bo-slee, and no other name will do. With the pronunciation of someone in the know, head to Honey Harbour, the terminal for water taxis serving cottagers and daytrippers in the 30,000 Islands.

A Beausoleil day, brand-new territory for most people, has a wonderfully adventurous feel to it. It is also a daytrip that requires a modicum of advance planning. First on the list is a call to a water taxi in Honey Harbour to arrange transport to and from the island; the best site on the island for drop-offs and pickups is a place called Cedar Spring. Second, prepare an ample picnic basket, for once on the island, you are on your own for supplies.

The fun starts as soon as your taxi, a powerful inboard/outboard, leaves the dock. Kids declare that the best part of a Beausoleil day is the taxi ride: wind and spray sting their faces, and the journey over the wake of huge power cruisers makes many amusement park rides pale in comparison. This is a good, inexpensive way to treat the family to a trip on the water. Honey Harbour is big boat country; Georgian Bay is abuzz with the sound and fury of gargantuan cruisers, sleek racing-boats and slow-lane houseboats crossing each other's wakes on all sides. In this unorchestrated ballet, water-taxi drivers are adept at finding their own passage, although they slow down and speed up at what seem to be invisible traffic intersections.

The taxi will drop you at Cedar Spring, which has several boat-in campsites, a picnic area and beach, and is handy to the park visitor centre and two self-guiding nature trails. Although the beach is very narrow, it is long and sandy. The south end of the beach area, near the visitor's centre, is a delightful place for a family swim. The water is very shallow a long way out, making it possible to walk to two small, rocky islands known as Squaw Rocks. There is a gentle but discernible water current over the boulders, and they are slippery with vegetation, but adventurers will insist that this only adds to the excitement.

 At the visitor's centre, in a small cabin near the beach, a slide show reviews the natural and human history of the island. Finds from an archaeological site indicate that the island was used as a temporary hunting and fishing camp at least 5,000 years ago. The discovery of a stone knife from Newfoundland proves that the Ojibwa from this region were linked to an incredibly wide trade network. The island was settled by loggers and farmers in the early years of the nineteenth century, but in 1929 it was bought by the federal government in order to protect the park from cottage development. Thus Beausoleil became the third national park in Eastern Canada.

Naturalists love to come to Beausoleil, because it is a place where northern and southern habitat types meet. This is strikingly evident on the nature trails: the northern end of the island has the granite and white pine one usually associates with Georgian Bay, while the southern end has deep, glacial soils that support maple, beech and ash. Beausoleil is home to 33 species of reptiles and amphibians (including the protected eastern massasauga rattlesnake), the highest number recorded for any park in Canada. Park staff lead daily hikes, and there is a special program for children.

You can pick up booklets to guide you along two trails close to Cedar Spring. Firetower Trail is an easy 1-kilometre loop that begins in open meadow cleared by Native settlers in the mid-1800s. Abundant wildflowers beautify the scene from spring to fall, and they attract many kinds of butterflies and birds. The trail enters a mature deciduous forest, where you will notice that the trees are especially large; this forest on Beausoleil represents one of the few areas in Southern Ontario that has not been logged.

The second trail, Bobbie's Trail, traverses a markedly different ecosystem. A series of ridges mark beaches that formed when glacial Lake Algonquin receded; these ridges have deep, damp hollows between them. The dry ridges are home to maple, birch and white-tailed deer, and the hollows support moisture-loving orchids, horsetails, ferns and mosses.

Beausoleil's trails are so enjoyable that it is easy to forget the time, but be sure to scurry back to the dock at Cedar Spring to rendezvous with your water taxi at the appointed hour.

Beausoleil Island, no matter how you pronounce it, is a guaranteed good day for the entire family.

Georgian Bay Islands National Park
Park open year-round
During the winter, visitor centre open
weekend afternoons only
(705) 756-2415

CnC Marina
(705) 756-3231

Admiral's Marina
(705) 756-2432

Honey Harbour Boat Club
(705) 756-2411

21 ELMVALE
Put a Spring in Your Step

Spring is a most exhilarating season. Mother Nature delivers an irresistible summons — cool breezes, maple sap and bird song — and young and old come forth to revel in fresh air and brilliant sunshine. Simcoe County rolls out the welcome mat for daytrippers anxious to celebrate the return of spring.

Begin the day early at Shaw's Pancake House. Drive northeast from Barrie on Highway 11; exit east at the Oro–Orillia Town Line and follow signs 2 kilometres to Shaw's. The Shaw family began maple syrup production in this bush 90 years ago. Although over the decades the equipment has evolved, from iron pots over an open fire to sophisticated evaporators, the sweet, golden product remains the same. Families and tour groups arrive to walk through the bush, learn about syrup production, and then savour maple treats at the long, gingham-covered tables in the restaurant. (Many visitors return in the fall to see the leaves.)

Brochures and explanatory signs tell all about sugar bush management and syrup production. Did you know, for example, that it takes five or six mature maples trees tapped continuously during the spring to produce a single gallon of syrup? Guests are allowed to watch the sap in the evaporator bubble its way to a satisfying conclusion. The restaurant specializes in pancakes, of course, but also serves maple baked beans, muffins with maple butter, and maple butter tarts. (During the fall, the menu features maple pumpkin pie.) Everything in the gift shop has to do with maple one way or another: clothing, recipe books, maple-syrup jelly, maple mustard, and maple barbecue sauce.

Now it's time to work off some of the tasty temptations of Shaw's. One of the best places to be in the springtime in Ontario is your nearest wetland, which in early spring is alive with the sound and motion of waterfowl. These creatures have a different notion of spring than we mammals: even though light snow and icy winds may make early April seem like winter to us, ducks and swans have already flown hundreds or thousands of kilometres to reach Southern Ontario.

One uncrowded and rewarding spot for spring nature-watching is little-known Tiny Marsh. From Shaw's, return to Highway 11 and drive southwest along 11 to Highway 27 and exit north-bound. Continue through Elmvale to where Highway 27 and County Road 6 form a Y-intersection, and drive along Road 6. Next, it's a west turn on Concession 1 (signposted), and then 4 kilometres further to Tiny Marsh Provincial Wildlife Area.

Tiny Marsh is 600 hectares of marsh and 300 hectares of field and forest. The interpretive centre, open spring and summer, has displays on wetlands, and hosts special events at the time of waterfowl migration. There are picnic shelters and washrooms.

Most visitors will head for the 8-kilometre trail system, which allows easy access to wooded swamps (habitat for muskrat and wood duck) and to dikes over-looking open water, just the place to watch for the first bufflehead, merganser or tundra swan of spring. The trails lead to observation blinds, towers and boardwalks; the centre supplies self-guiding brochures and a bird checklist. Although all appears to be just as nature designed it, Tiny Marsh is actually the result of active man-agement. Wildlife biologists built dams and dikes to control water levels and provided small islands and nest boxes to facilitate bird-nesting. In fact, this marsh was still farmland as recently as the mid-1960s, and the cooperation of the province and Ducks Unlimited turned it into much-needed wildlife habitat.

Tiny Marsh is well-suited for those unable to walk long distances, since the bird-watching is often good right beside the parking lot. Early-season swallows dip here to drink from the tiny canal, and yellow-rumped war-blers and kinglets flit in the bushes nearby.

Ontario's fickle spring weather can turn a planned day out-doors into a soggy and wind-whipped disaster. A good alternative is to look for signs of spring indoors, at Holt's Greenhouses. From

Tiny Marsh, return south on Highway 27 to Fergusonvale, a tiny community near the Phelpston Road intersection. Holt's is just north of this intersection.

A trip to Holt's Greenhouses during their marvellous spring floral display is a local pastime that is fast gathering visitors from far and wide. The rich perfume and dazzling colour of daffodils, tulips and hyacinth fill two greenhouses. As Easter approaches, thousands of lilies join the floral extravaganza. Many customers visit several times during the spring to watch their own special lily develop from a tiny shoot to a full-blossomed plant ready to take home.

The best time to visit Holt's is from about April 1 on, although earlier guests get to see the busy preparations for the spring display. Any time of the year, this is the spot for expert advice, and to pick up nursery stock and interesting gifts for gardeners.

Next time Mother Nature sends out her wake-up call, be sure to head for Simcoe County — with a spring in your step.

Shaw's Maple Products
March & April:
Daily 8–6
September–mid-October:
Weekends only
(705) 325-6878

Tiny Marsh
Daily, year-round
Seasonal hours at centre
(705) 322-2200

22 BARRIE
A Worthwhile Detour

To drivers headed north, Barrie represents the beginning of cottage country, or a convenient place to gas up before the fun begins. Barrie, however, has its own rewards for those with an interest in historic houses or a waterfront walk.

All roads in Barrie seem to head to Kempenfelt Bay, and so should daytrippers. Take the path that follows the curving shore of Kempenfelt Bay for a pleasant ramble. Centennial Beach, beloved by young and old for its sandy strand, gardens, picnic tables and snack bar, is also on the lakefront. You can pick up excellent Heritage Barrie walking-tour brochures that describe historic downtown buildings at the visitor centre, near the civic marina.

 Barrie has several neighbourhoods of interest to admirers of historic architecture. One of the most beautiful and pleasant for walking is just east of downtown. From the lakeshore, drive east along Dunlop (Barrie's main east-west street) to a fine pair of houses at numbers 158 and 162. The first was built in 1875 for a doctor, and the latter, a real beauty in the romantic, Queen Anne style, has a lookout from the third floor. Number 168 Dunlop is a lovely dark-brick home, rich with stained glass and polished woodwork inside. Once the home of a civic leader, Judge Donald Ross, it is now the Dove Restaurant. The Dove's entrees range from pasta to pheasant and include fresh local vegetables, and the service is always superb. This is a good point in your tour to abandon the car and become a pedestrian.

Continue along Dunlop, turn left at Berczy, then right at Collier. Many of the houses along Collier are now immaculately kept professional offices. Number 149 Collier was built in the neoclassical style, with a symmetrical facade and arched fanlights over the door. The house has a varied history, having served as a blacksmith's, saddlery, carriage shop and dairy — all at the same

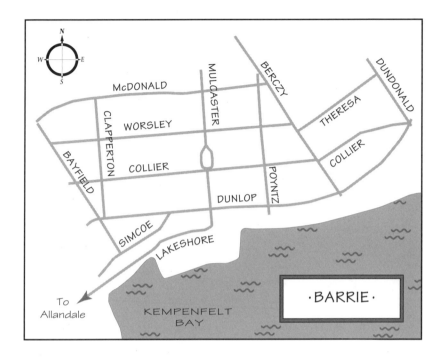

time. At Dundonald, turn left and walk uphill to Theresa, and then turn left again. Theresa Street is a tranquil walk. The magnificent two-toned brick mansion at number 33 was the home of mayor and MPP William Ardagh and was built in the 1870s. Head uphill again on Berczy, where many homes are sited diagonally on their lots to attain a bay view. Several have porches or gables turned at an angle to the rest of the house for the same reason; for example, see numbers 77, 83 or 89.

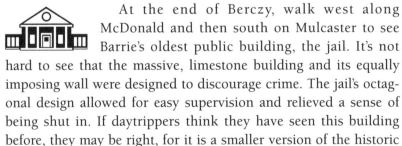
At the end of Berczy, walk west along McDonald and then south on Mulcaster to see Barrie's oldest public building, the jail. It's not hard to see that the massive, limestone building and its equally imposing wall were designed to discourage crime. The jail's octagonal design allowed for easy supervision and relieved a sense of being shut in. If daytrippers think they have seen this building before, they may be right, for it is a smaller version of the historic jail in Goderich.

This is the heart of public Barrie, and within a stone's throw of the jail are several buildings of note. Collier Street United Church (1864) is the church with the spire; this Gothic Revival building has a simple but appealing appearance. Its formality is in marked contrast to the more homespun charm of First Baptist Church, located just to the west at 37 Clapperton Street. This church was built in 1878 and has lovely ornamental brickwork, pointed windows, and a shingled turret.

Every Ontario downtown has at least one flatiron building, and Barrie's is the Simcoe Hotel (1876), at 31 Bayfield. The mansard roof is characteristic of Second Empire style. This is one of the notorious establishments that earned Barrie the reputation in the 1800s as the worst town for drink east of Winnipeg. Apparently, one of the reasons Barrie was known as a hard-drinking town was that it was a railway centre. You can discover more railway history just west of the downtown.

If you have been walking, return to the car and drive west along Lakeshore to the set of traffic lights at Tiffin; turn right to face the Thirsty Fox restaurant. This was once the "railway YMCA," where railroaders could get a cheap bed; it served in this capacity, supported by the Grand Trunk and the Canadian National Railway, until the 1950s. The Thirsty Fox menu features choices such as Ontario lamb osso buco, and duck legs with lingonberries.

Right across the street from the Thirsty Fox is the railway station built by the Grand Trunk in 1905. The style is Italianate, with wide, decorated eaves and an arcade. The ornate windows of the rounded waiting room commanded a view of the trains and the harbour. This part of town was originally Allandale, and most residents worked for the railway. You can still see some of their homes, often Second Empire duplexes or simple cottages, on the surrounding streets.

An afternoon perambulation along Barrie's elegant side streets is proof positive that we should plan on a long and congenial detour, instead of scurrying by on the highway.

23 BARRIE
Climb Every Mountain

Mountain biking has quickly become one of Ontario's most popular outdoor sports. Its advocates are usually members of the young and (very) fit set, who seek out hills and trails to master — the more difficult and dangerous, the better. Come to Hardwood Hills and find out that mountain biking is a tremendous sport for people of all ages and inclinations.

Hardwood Hills is a private sports facility designed especially for mountain biking in summer and cross-country skiing and snowshoeing in winter. It is very easy to find; just exit Highway 400 north of Barrie at Doran Road and drive east for 10 kilometres. Pay the very low all-day entry fee at the gate and then drive to the parking lot to unload the bikes, or to the chalet to rent Hardwood's bikes and helmets. Casual bikers who to try out the competition-quality bikes will be surprised to find the difference good equipment makes.

Excitement is in the air at Hardwood Hills even before you hit the trails. Seasoned athletes whiz down a steep, sandy hill into the parking lot; others fine-tune technical skills on the stairs, ramps and benches of an obstacle course. At first, it seems that no one here seems to consider straight-ahead biking a possibility. Don't be alarmed, there are trails for the novice. The least demanding is the Fun Trail, a good place to start for those who have never travelled off level, urban bike paths.

The Fun Trail begins on a wide roadway through mixed woods and ascends a couple of steep but very short hills before it heads into a mature pine plantation. The track narrows to shoulder width (at your shoulders, that is, but it is only centimetres wide at the ground), and curves between trees, stumps and rocks like a shoelace through eyelets. (Because of those stumps, you'll want to remove your kickstand for safety.)

By the end of the plantation section of the trail you will have the hang of steering, gearing and keeping your eyes on what's coming up, so that when you arrive back at the chalet you are proud of yourself, committed to further adventure.

Hardwood's more advanced trails have plenty to keep the most experienced rider challenged. They range in length from 10 to 14 kilometres, and are very tough physically and technically. Heart Attack Hill, Death Valley, Voorn's Vengeance, Roller Coaster Loop and the Grunt are just some of the trail nicknames. The trails are so good that Hardwood Hills is the site of the Canada Cup Mountain Bike events in 1996 and 1997.

This mountain-bike facility comes complete with bike wash, ever-ready mechanic, showers, supply and equipment shop, cafeteria (burgers and drinks), and picnic area. Expert staff run private and group clinics and lessons for all ages, as well as group events for businesses and clubs. There is a full slate of weekly races, divided according to trail, and the age and sex of entrants.

And if you thought mountain biking was fun, you'll be glad to know that the motto at Hardwood Hills is "learn to take winter in stride." Winter brings 30 kilometres of superbly groomed cross-country ski trails, from easy to challenging, equipment rentals and sales, and lessons from cross-country experts. This is Southern Ontario's only cross-country facility with complete snow-making, and some trails are lit at night. And Hardwood Hills has even opened up a "wilderness" area for bushwhacking skiers and snowshoers. Snowshoeing is enjoying a renaissance with those who like to leave the beaten track, and Hardwood Hills is prepared, with a line of snowshoes that can be used with their comfortable Salomon boots.

The best way to relax after a ski is to warm up in the chalet with some hot chocolate. During the summer biking season, the only way to really cool off is to head for the local swimming hole. The closest swimming to Hardwood Hills is at Bass Lake Provincial Park. Drive east on Doran Road (also known as Edgar–Rugby Road and Road 11), turn north at the 2nd Concession, and drive to the park entrance.

Bass Lake is a small, intensely used park that teems with family picnics and beach parties all summer long. Its beach, although busy, is a good place to recuperate after biking. Bass Lake is popular for fishing, and you can rent boats, canoes and fishing gear here. The Waterview Trail is a 3-kilometre hike through mixed forest and abandoned farm pastures.

One of the great things about mountain biking and cross-country skiing at Hardwood Hills is that there are trails for every skill and endurance level, and plenty of friendly expert advice and encouragement. No other facility makes it this easy, or fun, for every member of the family to climb their own mountain.

Hardwood Hills Cross Country Ski and Mountain Bike Centre
Biking
May–mid-November:
Monday–Friday 10–5
Saturday & Sunday 9–5
Skiing
December–mid-March:
Monday & Friday 9–4
Saturday & Sunday 8–5
Tuesday–Thursday 8–9
(705) 487-3775

24 PORT SEVERN
Best Trip by a Dam Site

O ntario, a land of lakes and rivers, is home to a great number of engineering marvels; we are connected by canals, hydro-electricity projects, bridges and tunnels. And one of these marvels, the Big Chute Marine Railway, makes for a daytrip combining good scenery, dining and a boat cruise.

You can may travel to Big Chute by land or by water, and there is room in a day for both ways. First, by water. Drive to Port Severn (north on Highway 69 and east at the Port Severn exit) and head for Bush's Boat Livery at the water's edge. The Bush family have worked with boats here for over a century, and there's not much they don't know about local history, either. Cruises to Big Chute depart daily at 2 PM and should be arranged by phone; groups are transported on a pontoon boat and individuals on a small cruiser.

The outings travel the length of Little Lake, squeeze in and around the islands heading into Gloucester Pool, cruise very close to the railway at Big Chute, and then return. This is very popular cottage and boating country, and the boat-channel is a veritable fashion show of marine technology. Cottage styles range from the classic, white-clapboard, green-shingle, Muskoka-chairs-on-the-lawn type to modern affairs with thousands of square metres of glass. Cruise guide Reg Bush provides details on some of the well-known personalities that belong to the cottages, and can also rattle off detailed information about the boats observed along the way — their design, manufacture and performance.

Before long, the cruise arrives at the marine railway, a long, flat railway car on tracks that lifts boats over a 17-metre wall of rock. Original plans were to have a standard lock at this site, but there were concerns that this would allow the spread of the dreaded lamprey eel. Thus, the Big Chute Marine Railway came into being, and it is the only such facility in the world. The railcar can carry several boats at a time, since its adjustable slings adapt to the size and shape of each boat. Boats are floated onto the railway from the waiting line in the lower basin, and then the railway begins its slow climb. As the dripping boats rise out of the water they appear a little ungainly, like sea creatures on dry land. They head out of sight at the top of the hill, and there's a wait before the train car appears with its downstream-headed load. The railway car stays almost level the whole trip due to a unique double-track system. The Bush cruise boat is allowed to come very close to the railway, so that the boats and the railway's mechanical underpinnings seem within reach.

The basin area is filled with large pleasure cruisers awaiting their turn to make the ascent. There are millions of dollars tied up in marine hardware here, and these floating homes have every possible convenience on board; it makes cruising the Trent–Severn Waterway look very comfortable indeed.

After the cruise, it's time for a meal. Port Severn may be a small community but it has three recommended eateries. Two are right in town: graceful Rawley Lodge, which has catered to tourists since 1927, and the Inn at Christie's Mill, a new arrival with a very popular Sunday brunch.

Perhaps the eating place with the longest his- tory is Severn Lodge. Drive north on Highway 69 to the White's Falls Road and follow signs to the lodge. The entrance of the main building is enticing: double French doors permit a view right through the lobby to the waters of Gloucester Pool. The lodge building was originally the bunkhouse and kitchen for the Georgian Bay Lumber Company, and was later a private fishing camp. Severn Lodge has been a tourist resort since the 1920s; its white and red cabins perched on a hill among the pine trees remain popular. Dinnertime menus feature delicacies such as coquilles cardinale (lobster and scallops in Remy Martin sauce), and turkey with ham dressing and leek and sherry sauce. Lunchtime guests enjoy salads, homemade soup and sandwiches, or can partake of the poolside barbecue.

After lunch, continue to drive east along  White's Falls Road to the parking lot at Big Chute. Explanatory signs on the grounds provide information on the railway's history and mechanical workings. Visitors can get a second very close look at the railway in action where it crosses the highway to unload boats at the upper waters. You can also walk down several flights of stairs to view the workings of the 1909 hydroelectric plant and dam, which have their own historical displays. The immediate vicinity is important ecologically, as it is home to at least 78 uncommon or rare plants and animals, among them the prairie warbler and massasauga rattlesnake; notice boards describe these species.

Ontario's engineering triumphs allow us to travel and communicate despite our lovely but challenging landscape. Some of these technical achievements can also be tourist attractions in their own right, as the Big Chute Marine Railway proves very satisfactorily.

Bush's Boat Livery
(705) 538-2378

Severn Lodge
(705) 538-2722

25 BALA
Muskoka's Rubies

There may not be gold in Muskoka's ancient hills, but there's something with much more appeal to tourists: rubies. Between sensational fall foliage and the cranberry harvest, Muskoka is distinctly red from mid-September to mid-October. Make the most of autumn's fine weather and take a tour through western Muskoka, beginning at Bala, 38 kilometres west of Gravenhurst on Highway 169.

Originally a mill town, Bala now caters to summer cottagers. The town has a great setting: the falls of the Moon River foam their way down rock ledges right in the centre of town. Take the time to park the car and walk to the falls to appreciate the thunder and mist. Sparkling stone Burgess Memorial Church (1926) is situated about as close to the falls as it can get without falling in. Just up the hill is cedar-shake Trinity St. Alban's Church. These two buildings are a part of what gives Bala Falls Road its rugged charisma.

Bala's reputation as the place to be in the fall comes from the humble cranberry. Cranberry vines thrive in Muskoka's acidic peat bogs, cool temperatures and abundant water. Bala hosts a cranberry festival every fall, the weekend after Thanksgiving; it includes art shows, a farmers' market, entertainment, and a cranberry breakfast at St. Alban's rectory. But if you prefer to avoid crowds, the cranberry harvest can be viewed anytime from late September through October.

Johnston's Cranberry Marsh and Iroquois Growers are Ontario's only commercial cranberry growers, and each sells 500,000 kilograms of berries annually. Johnston's is about 4 kilometres north of Bala; signs indicate a west turn off Highway 169 onto Medorra Lake Road. Johnston's offers a self-guiding brochure and, during the festival, short tours with a guide.

The marsh area is flat and low-lying, divided into growing sections by dikes. Visitors can saunter along these sandy dikes to observe the harvest. The growing areas are flooded to allow ripe berries to float, and then tiny, floating marsh "tractors" comb cranberries from the water and load them onto small barges to await pickup.

Johnston's store offers dozens of savoury cranberry products. There's juice of course, but also a variety of jams, jellies and chutney, from the lowly to the haute (cranberry pear sauce with port). Try the likes of cranberry vinegar, cranberry nut fudge, or cranberry honey jazz (fantastic for basting the turkey). There are also candles, pot pourri and cookbooks, all with a berry theme. Warm your hands around a cup of steaming, aromatic cranberry-apple cider.

 To find the Iroquois Growers, head back to Bala and west along Muskoka Road 38. This is a rewarding drive for fall leaves. When you reach Highway 69, drive north 5 kilometres to Iroquois Growers, operated by the Wahta Mohawks. Be sure to bring your camera; the marshes here are alive with animal life and surrounded by colourful forest. Vast numbers of cranberries are herded into a corner of each growing area — the water surface is completely covered — so you can fill your viewfinder completely with an intense red.

The main processing plant provides a close-up look at cranberry grading. Perfect berries bounce, but damaged or soft berries don't make it over the hurdles on the conveyors, and so drop out of the process. The retail counter here sells cranberry sauce, cordial, jams, and bags of berries.

Return to Bala. Before leaving town along Highway 169 north, you may want to pick up a snack at Don's Bakery. Follow that heady scent of yeast and brown sugar to find a good selection of hearty breads, sweet buns and squares. At tiny Glen Orchard, turn east on Highway 118 for a colour tour around Lake Muskoka.

Each bend in the highway brings a vista more breathtaking than the last. Muskoka leaves are redder than those anywhere else in the province, and the landscape seems tailor-made for scenery hunters. Crimson, gold and russet stand in sharp contrast to rocky, grey outcrops, deep green pine, and white birchbark. An artist couldn't arrange things for better effect.

Just when you think you've seen about as much gorgeous landscape as you can handle, the Huckleberry rock-cut near Milford Bay comes into sight. Park the car, stretch your legs, and have a look at Ontario's longest highway rock-cut. The scene in either direction is of a long pink rock corridor that leads to orange forest, framed with pine.

The last beauty spot before ending the tour at Bracebridge is a long bay of Lake Muskoka that shimmers deep blue, undisturbed by summertime boaters. In order to fully savour the prospect, stop for a meal at Tamwood Lodge, a log inn built in the late 1930s. The dining room enjoys a fine lake view, and the warm gleam of the log interior and the stone hearth will chase away any autumn chill. Dining at Tamwood is very popular, especially the Friday night buffets and the twice-weekly barbecues during the summer.

Locals have it right when they say that autumn in Muskoka is crantastic!

Johnston's Cranberry Marsh
(705) 762-3203

Iroquois Growers
(705) 762-3343

Tamwood Lodge
(705) 645-5172

26 PORT CARLING
Grand Old Holidays

Picture this: a wide, white verandah framed by bright flowers and pine trees; wooden rocking chairs swaying slightly in the cooling breeze; French doors opened onto a dining room where fine china and silverware gleam on starched linens. Now put yourself in the picture by way of a daytrip to two of Muskoka's hotels that were, and still are, grand places to visit.

Drive north on Highway 11, and then west on Highway 118. At Muskoka Road 7, turn north toward Minett. Follow signs to Clevelands House, the grandest resort in Muskoka. The resort was established in the mid-nineteenth century when the owners, early settlers for whom the town of Minett was named, took guests into their home.

The main lodge building has a wide, wraparound verandah, and balconies that rise in tiers like layers on a wedding cake. Red, green and yellow Muskoka chairs sit in an orderly row on the lawn, flowers grow lushly in well-tended gardens; and cabanas line the beach. Clevelands' hundreds of hectares are home to a golf course, 16 tennis courts, pools, badminton and basketball courts, exercise rooms and a marina. The celebrated children's program runs from a playground and activity centre larger than some amusement parks.

A typical lunch at Clevelands includes beef stroganoff, baked sugar-cured ham with mango sauce, and chicken salad croissant. Sunday is barbecue day, when lunch is served buffet-style in a large tent on the lawn. Dinnertime brings poached Canadian salmon with dill sauce or grilled breast of capon with a julienne of fresh vegetables, followed by raspberry peach pie, hazelnut cake or New York cheesecake.

Return to Highway 118 and turn west to Glen Orchard and the Sherwood Inn (1939). This tranquil resort is not as old nor as grand as Clevelands House, but it has the appeal of an elegant country inn and is recommended for lunch today. The inn is a sedate white building with green shutters and awnings, and brick walkways bordered by impatiens. The main lounge, with stone fireplace and comfy sofas, exemplifies the entire resort: relaxed, but classy. There is a beach here, and guests can take part in many activities, including watersports, volleyball, badminton, shuffleboard, croquet and billiards. Sherwood, unlike many cottage country inns, is open year-round, and in winter offers 16 kilometres of ski trails, and skating, ice fishing and broomball.

 Sherwood's kitchen is renowned for its excellence in preparation and service, so much so that the inn organizes country cooking weekends for the gourmet. Dinner might be Atlantic salmon in pastry, served with a horseradish hollandaise, or a blanquette of king scallops and Gulf shrimp on saffron ravioli with cucumber and star anise. Dessert may be a hot pancake moneybag filled with poached pear, brie and kumquat marmalade. Many resorts have an uninspired lunch menu, but Sherwood's midday repast is worth raving about; you could be choosing from curried shrimp or a warm salad of grilled Provençal vegetables, followed by crème brûlé or maple-syrup mousse.

After a pleasant repast at the Sherwood, drive east to the hub of the Muskoka Lakes, Port Carling. Spend some time in the shady park that overlooks the locks and the daily float-past of sailboats, catamarans and power cruisers. The Muskoka Lakes Museum stands on the knoll in the centre of the park. Artifacts, text, maps, and photographs tell the story of boats, boatbuilding, and the settlement of the area. If you're wondering where the well-to-do of Muskoka shop, it's probably Port Carling. Two favourite stores are the Muskoka Moose, for brilliantly coloured papier-mâché trays and bentwood baskets, and the Port Carling Bakery, for — where else but in Muskoka — chocolate boats.

It's time to pay our respects to one of Muskoka's grand old dames, Windermere House. From Port Carling drive north on Road 25, then west on Road 24 to Windermere. At the time this book was printed, lovely Windermere had just burned to the ground. In its day it was an enormous version of classic Muskoka, an expanse of gleaming white wood, red shingles, red-and-white striped awnings over gabled windows, and a central, flag-topped tower. High society stayed in the original lodge in the 1870s, and it was easy to imagine guests, servants and luggage arriving by steamship. No doubt there are already interesting plans underway for this treasured piece of Muskoka waterfront.

One is allowed to be a little wistful when leaving the magic of old Muskoka for a return to the modern world. The air of grand holidays from the bygone era of steamships and dressing for dinner is rather addictive, so be prepared to make another escape to stately resorts and fine cuisine soon.

Sherwood Inn
(705) 765-3131

Clevelands House
(705) 765-3171

27 SEGUIN FALLS
Ride the Ghost Train

Lumber baron and railroad magnate J.R. Booth was a colourful character about a century ago, at a time when Central Ontario was the wild and woolly domain of logger and miner. Booth's fervour for business expansion led him to push a railroad through the wilderness from his Ottawa mills to Georgian Bay. Take a day to explore the intriguing remains of those frontier days, in the form of a wilderness railway and a ghost town. The best way to do this is to travel to the greater Parry Sound tourist region and cycle along the Seguin Trail, Booth's old railbed turned into a recreational trail. The trail begins at Highway 69, 6 kilometres south of Oastler Lake Provincial Park, and runs east 61 kilometres to reach Fern Glen, close to Highway 11.

Commence at the western end of the trail. (Parking and trail guides are available at the nearby tourist information centre.) Although the path cuts through hilly Canadian Shield terrain, it is relatively undemanding because it started out as a railbed, and trains cannot handle extremely steep hills. How pleasant to travel along several undeveloped lakes, refuges for loons and other creatures increasingly unwelcome farther south. Take the time to observe a beaver at work, or a northern harrier on the hunt. The only sounds are your footsteps or tires, and the tinkling of the streams and waterfalls that run alongside, underneath and across the trail.

The trail surface is packed earth and gravel, with some boulder sections where washouts have prompted repair. These are often located on the few hilly runs there are, and can make for enjoyable mountain biking. Springtime washouts can be quite deep, so phone the Ministry of Natural Resources Office for an up-to-date report on trail conditions. The only decision you need to make is whether to cycle the entire 61 kilometres to the eastern end of the trail (overnight camping is permitted), or to go for a shorter ride and return to the start point to travel some of that distance by car.

If you return to the car, drive north on Highway 69 and head east on Highway 518. (Don't worry, we meet up with Mr. Booth's railway again soon enough.) Highway 518 winds and climbs its way through woods and pasture and passes by isolated schools and homesteads. Be prepared for a southward turn marked for Seguin Falls, about 30 kilometres east of Highway 69 at the Nipissing Road.

The Nipissing Road was one of Ontario's infamous colonization roads, intended to open up the wilderness to settlement. Most colonists left, beaten by the isolation, intense poverty and bedrock. Small settlements such as Seguin Falls developed along these "roads of disappointed hopes" to provide creature comforts for stagecoach passengers. When Booth's railway crossed the Nipissing Road a few kilometres to the south of town, the town centre also moved; with the addition of enterprises such as a mill, and a school and church, the town flourished. Good times continued right up to the 1920s, when lumbering declined and the few remaining farmers pulled up stakes.

Slow the car as you approach Seguin Falls in order to glimpse the tumbling white waters that gave this tiny settlement its name; the best vantage point is from near the farm at the bend in the road. This is a fabulous setting for a ghost town, and rates some exploration by foot. Not a soul is about but the wind, which rustles the aspen and asters that are gradually reclaiming old building sites. It makes a good picnic site for today's lunch.

What signs do we have of Seguin Falls today? Near the Sequin Trail is the King George Hotel, now a residence, in its heyday a home for loggers and a general store. The school also has become a private residence, and most other buildings are vacant. A few cabins in and around town, and grave markers along the Nipissing Road are mute witnesses to the hardships of the frontier.

Readjust your mental clock to the 1990s and return to Highway 518. Turn east if you want to try your legs along the eastern section of the Seguin Trail, which may be picked up at Jarlsberg (Bear Lake) or just east of Sprucedale. (Keep an eye out for the white signs that mark where the trail crosses the highway.) From Jarlsberg it is about 24 kilometres to the trail end at Fern Glen. The eastern part of the trail is very flat, and for those who do not appreciate biking in sand, not as much fun as the western end. The trail does have its rewards for those who persevere, however, as it travels through the heart of several large wetlands. What a thrill it is to be the only person in sight, surrounded by dogwood and cattails, with kilometres of wilderness ahead. No wonder this section of the trail is a highlight for many bikers. (A word of caution: wetlands mean mosquitoes and black flies in season; be prepared to use bug spray or to pedal fast!)

Whether you tackle the Seguin Trail in one ride, or use the car to sample part of it, one and all will agree that Booth's railway is still the best way to visit the frontier.

28 ORILLIA
Summer Side of Life

Peonies in full, fragrant bloom... the slow arc of a well-cast line... the creak of a rocking chair on a wide verandah... the rippled reflection of a sailboat in a quiet bay. Orillia is Ontario's archetypal vacation town, best visited during the long days of summer when time seems to stand still.

A good place to ease into a holiday state of mind is the home of Orillia's most famous native son, Stephen Leacock. Drive to Orillia on Highway 11, exit at Highway 12, and stay on Highway 12 until it reaches Atherley Road near the lakeshore. Turn left onto Atherley, right on Forest Avenue, and follow signs to the Stephen Leacock Museum.

Take a leisurely stroll around Leacock's 40-hectare property and you'll feel as if you've stepped back 60 years. The 19-room cottage by the water was built in 1928 and was used by Leacock until his death in 1944. It was here, in a room over the boathouse, that Leacock wrote several of his best works. Many personal effects are on display, including original manuscripts with his own editorial comments, and a good number of charming photographs of the man with the wry smile, and text on his career. What does a man trained in economics but best known as a humourist read? Visit the library to find his very own 5,000-volume collection, which extends from *Pilgrim's Progress* to *The Dictionary of Political Economy*.

The cottage portrays much more than the life and work of Leacock; it is a charming example of a lifestyle of simple luxury in Ontario's vacationland. Perennial borders are richly perfumed with old-fashioned favourites such as roses and peonies, and there's a tree-framed view of the moored boats and sunning mal-

lards on Brewery Bay. Inside, the cottage gleams with the warmth of aged wood, the table is set for tea, and tennis racquets and fishing rods wait by the door. It may seem a pity to leave the Leacock property, but leave you must, for the many other attractions of Orillia await.

Drive into town along Atherley Road and park the car near the town dock at the foot of Mississauga Street. Walk uphill to explore the Mariposa Market, a collection of shops in a century-old general store complete with tin ceiling and hardwood floors. High-quality goods, engaging surroundings and friendly service make this stop a shopping highlight of cottage country.

The main-floor café turns out inventive dishes such as chicken Kiev sandwiches and maple-apple-walnut swirls. Authentic blackballs, jawbreakers and horehound make the candy department a trip down memory lane. The store's floor-to-ceiling shelves are stocked with an assortment of items to decorate the kitchen, from ceramic vegetables to specialty serving dishes. On Mariposa Market's lower level, the love of food continues, with a plethora of handy gadgets, from pumpkin knives to ginger graters, and unique gift ideas such as beer bread mix (complete with baking dish, mix and instructions) and homemade truffles (regular and dietetic items). The Scent Shop offers a surfeit of dainty items from Crabtree & Evelyn, natural soaps and Victorian lingerie. The Kids Clothing Company can help send Junior out into the world well-dressed.

Just uphill from the Mariposa Market stands the stately, redbrick Orillia Opera House. It hosts a summer schedule of light theatre and musicals.

Head downhill to the town dock, the departure point for the Island Princess cruise boat. Two-hour cruises depart twice daily during the summer, and there are popular roast beef and barbecue trips Thursday through Saturday evenings. The cruise boat is a good vantage point for a photograph of Orillia, the brilliant turquoise water of Lake Couchiching occupying the foreground and, onshore, church steeples and the opera house tower poking through the leafy canopy.

The information-packed cruise narrative covers local history, from the earliest settlements of 10,000 years ago to modern times.

Sights en route include the Leacock home, a Victorian bandshell, the Champlain Monument, and well-known Fern Resort and Geneva Park. And then there's "Bay Street," a stretch of summer mansions belonging to the elite of Toronto's business community. (Note the biplanes moored at the docks.)

Stay in a summer state of mind by dining near the waterfront. Handsome old train cars have been given a new lease on life as the Ossawippi Express Dining Cars, located just across the street from the marina. The train cars include the 1896 parlour car employed as the official executive coach of the Nova Scotia Government, and an electric interurban train from 1905 complete with Tiffany glass and solid brass fittings. They make an appropriate setting for the likes of carrot-ginger bisque, cranberry chicken pita, and rich strawberry-chocolate crepes.

A day in Orillia is a celebration of fine gardens, waterside scenery and the relaxed pace of a small town ... a walk on the summer side of life.

Stephen Leacock Museum
Mid-June–mid-September:
Daily 10–7
Call for other hours
(705) 326-9357

Orillia Boat Cruises
July–September:
Saturday–Thursday 11 & 2
Thursday–Saturday 6:30 (dinner cruise)
May, June & September: weekends
(705) 325-2628

Osssawippi Express Dining Cars
(705) 329-0001

29 GRAVENHURST
Riding the Mails...

The Royal Mail Ship *Segwun*, that is. This beloved vessel symbolizes everything gracious about the days when Muskoka was a summer retreat for the wealthy. Steamships such as the *Segwun* carried mail, supplies, cottagers and servants throughout the lakes. It is a special treat to take a cruise on the *Segwun*, the finest reminder of the great era of steam in North America.

Drive to Gravenhurst by way of Highway 11 and follow the steamship signs to the *Segwun* dock, where there is a small museum, park and ticket office. Select a cruise from the diverse offerings, from simple sightseeing trips to all-day extravaganzas that feature lunch at a grand old resort. Best of all may be the Millionaires' Row cruise, which sails three times a week to Beaumaris, playground of the rich for over a century. Be sure to call ahead and make reservations. (And keep in mind that the *Segwun* provides Thanksgiving and fall-foliage season weekend packages.)

The 40-metre *Segwun* was constructed in 1887 as a side-wheeled paddle steamer for the Muskoka Navigation Company. The iron hull was cast in the Clyde shipyards in Scotland. The *Segwun* stills sails under the insignia of that fleet, and it is that insignia that appears on mail posted on board and on the ship's china. This is the last authentic steamship still in operation on the continent, and it sails with a crew of 11 and about 90 passengers.

What a sight the *Segwun* makes as it approaches the dock, immaculately tailored in white and green, a black cloud billowing from the stack. Once on board, surrounded by gleaming woodwork and brass fittings, it is easy to imagine away the decades and picture elegant ladies in long linen skirts leaning against the rails.

 Steam-engine buffs head to the open engine room to watch its smooth operation. There's even a grate in the floor so visitors can watch the crew serve up

Segwun's rations of West Virginia coal. It is only after being on board awhile that you appreciate *Segwun*'s quiet operation: the cruise is an auditory pleasure as well as a visual one.

The open deck provides glorious views of typical Muskoka scenery and cottages galore. Some are simple log cabins, others are modern chalets; but those that garner a collective sigh from the passengers are the Victorian mansions, up to 600 square metres in size, with boathouses of equal elegance. The captain's narration provides details on cottage age, design, local history, and occasionally on the families fortunate enough to vacation here. The *Segwun* is a respected local citizen, and when cottagers and their pets come to their docks to wave, wag and bark hello, they are answered with a quick blast on the horn.

The dining room has a curving bank of windows, which means that the sightseeing doesn't end at dinner. Some lucky passengers are assigned to the private "captain's dining room," which seats only two and is located at the opposite end of the ship from the main dining room. *Segwun*'s kitchen prepares hot rolls, salad, prime rib cooked to perfection, a julienne of fresh local vegetables and a crumb-topped blueberry pie.

On returning to Gravenhurst, visit the Heritage Centre, for its exhibits on the age of steamships and local boatbuilders, and to buy souvenir clothing and books in the gift shop. Then head into town to learn of Gravenhurst's other celebrated citizen, Norman Bethune. Follow signs to his birthplace at the corner of John and Hughson Streets.

Main-floor rooms have been furnished in the style of the late 1800s, the period when Bethune's father was minister at nearby Knox Church. The second floor is devoted to the compelling story of Bethune's career as a doctor on the field in the First World War, the Spanish Civil War (where he developed a mobile blood-transfusion system), and the Sino-Japanese War. It was in China that Bethune established hospitals, trained doctors, invented a mobile operating theatre, and thereby won the admiration of the Chinese. His career was marked by untiring and selfless devotion to the alleviation of suffering; he performed a record 115 operations in 69 hours while under heavy artillery fire in China. Bethune also had a knack for flamboyance and controversy, and fought hard for socialized medicine long before it became an acceptable notion.

Gravenhurst has other attractions to round out your day. Several buildings along the main street bear large murals that depict scenes from local history. A descriptive brochure is available at the Opera House (1897), the large redbrick building with the corner tower at the centre of downtown Gravenhurst. The Opera House is the home of Muskoka Festival's summer performances of comedy, drama and musicals.

A cruise on the RMS *Segwun* is one of the continent's most romantic holiday adventures. Don't miss the opportunity to put yourself into history by "riding the mails," Muskoka-style.

Muskoka Lakes Navigation
(705) 687-6667

30 BRACEBRIDGE
Just Kiddin' Around

It's all too easy to plan a vacation around adult pursuits and forget that kids need to have their day as well. This attitude can quickly lead to back-seat revolts. Under such circumstances, centrally located Bracebridge, with its assortment of attractions sure to please the young, and the young at heart, is the holiday town to head for.

Bracebridge is the home of Santa's Village. The route from Highway 11 is well posted. Santa's Village comprises two areas: the original village, geared to small fry, and newer Rudolph's Funland, designed with older kids and young teens in mind.

First on the agenda should be the village proper and the amusement park rides for the little ones: Rudolph's Sleigh Ride (a scream for young and old riders), the Candy Cane Express Train, Christmas Ball Ferris Wheel, Red Baron Planes and the Christmas Carousel. But there's much more than just rides — kids can play minigolf, explore the river on a paddlewheeler, cruise the lagoon in a pedal boat, bump boats with their siblings in the boat corral, swim at the beach, and play with remote-control boats. They can meet Santa and the elves and the herd of deer (not a single red nose here on Santa, or the deer). There are small souvenir stands to burn a hole in that hard-earned allowance money, as well as snack bars, ice-cream stands, and Mrs. Claus's Gingerbread House. (Where does she find the time?)

Older children will be chomping at the bit to head for Rudolph's Funland, where the activities are more sophisticated and require a certain measure of skill. Funland has a half-kilometre track for go-carts, 18-hole minigolf, batting cages, and pathways for inline skating (skate rentals are available, or bring your own). And Santa has gone high-tech with his newest attraction, Laser Storm, an interactive laser tag game.

The farm at Santa's Village has animals to pet and pony rides; the playground has gigantic cargo nets, ball crawls and other calorie-burning delights: and for those more worldly members of the family, there are games arcades. Daily performances by children's entertainers take place at the outdoor theatre.

Bracebridge has other winning attractions for families. Eco-kids will want to head for the Bracebridge Natural Resource Management Centre on Highway 11 just north of town. Be on the lookout for the small sign on the right-hand side of the highway. These 600 hectares were once logged, farmed and used as a deer sanctuary, but are now primarily for hikes and skiing. The main trail is well marked, as is a side trail leading to a lookout over rapids on the Muskoka River. A word to the entomophobic: the resource management centre is very definitely mosquito-friendly. Repellent is required all summer long, and on some days the bugs will either cut short a hike or keep you moving at a brisk pace.

Kids with a more urban attitude will probably be happy to skip the hike and head for downtown. Bracebridge's downtown is compact, so the recommended strategy is to find a parking spot and leave the car. Children and their parents love the Factory Store at 41 Manitoba Street, the main street of town. It advertises itself as the largest manufacturer of heat transfers for printing sportswear in Canada. Over 800 designs are displayed on the walls and in central racks, filed according to subject. Just pick a transfer, pick an item of clothing (sweatshirts, sweatpants, T-shirts and nightshirts in all sizes and colours), and take them to the counter for production. The prices are so reasonable that a family could outfit themselves for back-to-school all in one visit.

Manitoba Street has loads of craft, decorating and clothing stores to occupy any shopper, so browse a bit as you walk down toward the river. (En route, let the kids have a spree in the dollar bargain store.) At the river, head for the Bird's Mill Building, originally part of the woollen mill owned by local entrepreneur Henry Bird, and now housing an attractive complex of stores and a café.

It's the café that is the point of this riverside sojourn, and the kids will applaud this choice of eatery when they get a load of the sweets. You won't find goodies like these — black flies (cookies with chocolate bits) and moose droppings (pure chocolate lumps) — anywhere else. The sweets are produced at nearby Maple Orchard Farms/The Chocolate House. If you have a need to see the production process, ask at the café for directions. Adults may want to know that the café can also supply the rest of a balanced diet, and that its scenic location beside the waterfall makes it a good choice for a meal.

Bracebridge is tailor-made for just kiddin' around.

Santa's Village & Rudolph's Funland
Mid-June–September:
Daily
In addition, Rudolph's Funland is open mid-May–mid-June:
Weekends
(705) 645-2512

31 BRACEBRIDGE
History Is for the Birds

A history lesson made pleasurable — that's one of the most endearing accomplishments of Bracebridge. Every community has its own story to tell, its own heroes and villains, triumphs and tragedies. Bracebridge has decided to capture and present its history in a way that resident and tourist alike can enjoy.

The dark, swirling Muskoka River runs through the centre of town, and it is at the riverside where the story of Bracebridge begins. Downstream from the fabulous falls the river widens, and around this widening, called Bracebridge Bay, there is a walking path. Along the path are storyboards that use not only words to describe events but go one better and supply historic photographs showing exactly what you would be looking at from the same spot, decades ago. Park the car downtown, or on the opposite side of the river in a small park, and walk the entire informative route.

The first storyboard tells how this bay was a portage route for Ojibwa hunters and, later, David Thompson of the North West Company (1837). Other storyboards provide details on lumber and shingle mills (1880s), the construction of the Northern Railway (1885), and the advent of municipally owned hydroelectric power in Ontario when Bracebridge purchased a small station from W.S. Shaw (1892). The picturesque pumping station with its floral window-boxes and pastel painted exterior not only survives; it remains the backup system for the town water supply.

Such intense industrial development doesn't occur without the genius and ambition of great entrepreneurs, and Bracebridge had its own in the person of Henry James Bird. Bird bought a mill in 1872 and began the production of high-quality woollen goods. Famous Bird coats, used largely by lumbermen and the military, were produced in this riverside mill until the mid-1950s, when less-expensive synthetic materials became popular.

Bird was successful not only in business but in community life, and the town has shown its gratitude by maintaining Bird's home, Woodchester Villa (built in 1882 and affectionately called the Bird Cage), as a museum. Follow the marked pathway from the river up a hill to Woodchester. Before you enter the house, be sure to turn and take in the view Henry Bird would have had of the town and mills laid out at his feet.

Woodchester is not just a monument to Bird and the development of early Bracebridge, but also an interesting example of an uncommon school of house design advocated by American Orson Fowler. Woodchester Villa is octagonal in shape, is constructed of poured concrete, and has a wraparound porch and balcony and an interior layout arranged to maximize ventilation. Given typical living conditions in Muskoka at the time, many features of this house, such as forced-air heating, indoor plumbing, electrical lighting, a speaking tube and dumb waiter, would have been considered avant-garde.

Guides host informative tours of the fully furnished house; it includes a formal parlour, a dining room with mahogany Jacques & Hayes furniture, kitchen, bedrooms and Bird's home office. Mrs. Bird's own wedding dress is laid out on the bed in the master bedroom, and the office looks as if Henry is still using it. It features a built-in desk and shelves (how else to deal with a triangular room?) and a direct telephone line to the mill. Muskoka Arts and Crafts and its art gallery are located in a separate building on the grounds of Woodchester Villa.

Walk back down the hill and cross the river. The pedestrian walkway directly over the falls is as close as you'll get to the awesome power of a big river. The river just below your feet is smooth black glass until it hits the falls, where it roars and cascades as a white froth. This is one of the most-photographed scenes in all Muskoka. Continue along the west side of the bay for more great storyboards.

After a day immersed in old-time Bracebridge, it is apropos to walk up the hill on the west side of the river to dine at Inn at the

Falls, which dates to the 1870s. This romantic, white frame building has three dining areas. The downstairs pub, the Fox & Hounds, is a perfect place to warm yourself by the fire after a winter walk. It offers a diverse range of salads, sandwiches, a ploughman's lunch and fresh fruit pies. During the summer, dine on the patio with its lovely river view, or in the formal dining room, Victoria's. Dinner may start with Muskoka trout pâté and then move on to seafood Wellington or chicken in a peach schnapps sauce. "Turtle" pie and meringue Victoria (a swirl of meringue with ice cream, raspberry sauce and whipped cream) are examples of the Inn's decadent desserts.

If only history were taught in school the way Bracebridge teaches it along the heritage walkway. What an enjoyable way to learn about the past.

Woodchester Villa
(705) 645-8111

32 HUNTSVILLE
Northern Traditions

It's remarkable that a region as recently developed as Muskoka could be so steeped in tradition. Most settlement has occurred in the past century, and yet, as today's journey illustrates, some Muskoka scenes and customs have been around for so long, they appear to be a permanent part of the locale.

Exit Highway 11 at Muskoka Road 3 to Huntsville; Road 3 becomes Main Street. Turn right at Brunel Road and follow signs to the Muskoka Pioneer Village. Many Ontario towns have pioneer villages, but what is different about Huntsville's is that the buildings here, backwoods cabins and two-storey frame houses, are not much different from those seen along country byways throughout Muskoka. The region is not that far removed from its pioneer origins.

The main museum describes regional history through text, maps and photos. Fourteen build-ings have been arranged as a typical nineteenth-century community. Home life is portrayed in the Darling's tiny log cabin, the more comfortable farmhouse of the Hares, and the substantial two-storey home of Reverend Hill. "Downtown" Muskoka centres on the Spence Inn (temperance, of course), the Hay General Store, Wesley Church and the Orange Hall. Costumed staff recreate the work and play of pioneer days, and visitors are encouraged to participate.

The village really comes alive for a strawberry social in July, a market day, with music and refreshments, in August, and Victorian Christmas in December. In February the smell of wood fires fills the air as chefs from nearby Deerhurst Resort serve up delicious pancakes and hot syrup.

Drive north to Highway 60 and turn east. Exit south at Muskoka Road 23. The road winds through forest, and at a sharp bend in the road, the Portage Inn appears as a small oasis of creature comforts. On the shoreline nearby is a wharf that served the "world's smallest railway," which linked Lake of Bays to the south with Peninsula Lake. (For the full story of the railway, read *Explore Muskoka* by Susan Pryke.) Park by the water just along Road 23, at South Portage, and take in the sight of the deep blue of Lake of Bays. (The land here was filled in over the remains of the steamboat Iroquois.)

 Continue the fine backroad drive south along Muskoka Road 9 where Lake of Bays peeks out from between cottages and birch trees. The next village is Baysville, which at one time was a busy lumber town, but is now more popular for its riverside park and dam. Should you decide to wet your whistle in the tavern across the street from the park at the dam, you will be joining in a tradition that goes back over a century among hunters and fishermen. Visit another local tradition, Langmaid's Store, just down the street; it also dates back to pioneer days. One Baysville old-timer that is still around is St. Ambrose Anglican Church, which sits on a hill just above the village, keeping company with the original wooden schoolhouse.

From Baysville drive east on Highway 117 toward Dorset. For one especially interesting detour, follow the road marked Norway Point Church to the water's edge, turn right and drive along to reach this charming little white church.

 Return to the highway to Dorset, and look for Lake of Bays Park (a parking lot and boat launch). From the shore, look across to Bigwin Island, but don't rub your eyes! That is not a mirage, that is indeed a huge, abandoned resort complex. Bigwin Inn was constructed between 1910 and 1920 and served an elite international clientele until the mid-1940s. So far the story is like that of several other grand old Muskoka hotels. Unlike some others that have burned down or have been demolished, however, the Bigwin is still completely intact, and from the shore you can see the rounded dining-room, waterfront and dance hall.

Drive east to Dorset, a small town that overlooks the waterway between Lake of Bays and Johnnycake Bay. Many people are familiar with Robinson's General Store, voted Canada's best country store. Step inside for feather dusters, minnows, afghans, coffee pots, coonskin hats, flannel nightgowns and a can of beans — all the usual cottage requirements. Dorset has several gift shops, and more than its share of recommended eateries, including the Tom Salmon Inn and the Cedar Narrows Restaurant.

The last event of the day is a climb up Dorset's fire tower on Highway 35 north of town. The climb will be difficult for those unaccustomed to heights or climbing, but the view is worth it. Lake of Bays and little Dorset are down below you, and a hilly carpet of green stretches to the horizon. During the fall foliage season, the fire tower is on the itinerary of many daytrippers for the Sunday drive in the country.

Take a daytrip to Huntsville and the Lake of Bays and find out first-hand that enjoyable traditions don't take centuries to evolve. In fact, you can make countryside rambles among Muskoka's northern lakes a personal tradition of your own.

Muskoka Pioneer Village
Village buildings
July & August: Daily 10–5
Museum building
As above, and also
September–mid-October:
Monday–Friday 10–4:30
(705) 789-7576

33 HUNTSVILLE
Banish the Winter Blahs

Dust off the toboggan, sharpen the skates, and dig out the long underwear: it's time to banish the winter blahs for good! Head for the winter paradise known as Huntsville and take in a day of outdoor therapy guaranteed to revitalize and refresh.

The first stop of the day is Arrowhead Provincial Park, located 8 kilometres north of Huntsville on Highway 11. While some parks are closing up for the winter, the fun is just starting at Arrowhead. There are two centres of activity, Mayflower Lake and Arrowhead Lake, and each site has its own parking lot, warm-up shelter and washrooms.

The biggest attraction is the toboggan hill at Mayflower Lake. There's no need to navigate; just follow the shrieks of delight that echo through the snow-blanketed woods. The toboggan run occupies a steep, unploughed road, with one side for sliders and one side for those puffing their way back up the hill. The run is about half a kilometre long, with a couple of fast curves. Just as you are bracing yourself for a crash over the bank and into the forest, gravity comes to the rescue and pulls you back to safety. Bring your own toboggan or make use of equipment supplied free of charge by the Ministry of Natural Resources. Choose between gigantic inner-tubes (nice cushions for the timid) and long rolls of plastic that can take the whole party in one sitting.

After catching your breath and warming up in the picnic shelter, try out the trails. The Mayflower Lake Activity Area is the starting point for three cross-country ski trails; they range in length from 2.7 to 3 kilometres and in terrain from level to steep and rugged. The Arrowhead Lake Activity Area features three ski trails, including the 1-kilometre Bunny Trail for children. The 4-kilometre East River Trail leads to an overlook high above the meandering Big East River, and the 9-kilometre

Beaver Meadow Trail is recommended for observing wildlife. Both of these trails are suitable for intermediate and advanced skiers. All ski trails are track-set and groomed daily, and there are ski rentals and sales at the park office.

For those who prefer to walk in a winter wonderland, the 1.6-kilometre Stubb's Falls snowshoe and hiking trail begins at the bridge over the Little East River near the Arrowhead Activity Area and follows a maple-cedar-birch ravine to the falls. In winter the quiet is disturbed only by the squeak of snow underfoot and the friendly *chick-a-dee-dee* call. Stubb's Falls is a mini-Niagara; where the torrent of water surges through a narrow chasm the rocky walls are draped with a thick layer of ice.

For more winter fun, go on the ice. Mayflower and Arrowhead Lakes are stocked with trout, and park staff will suggest the most productive locations for ice fishing. There is a small skating rink near the Mayflower Activity Area.

You can enjoy a whole day full of outdoor fitness and fun at Arrowhead, but there is still more to see in the vicinity. Huntsville has the second-highest snowfall in the province (over 300 centimetres on average), and that means Hidden Valley Highlands is the place to go for a long season of skiing and snowboarding. The prices for passes and rentals are reasonable, and skiers can enjoy night skiing and lessons, and refuel at the cafeteria and lounge. Hidden Valley is located off Highway 60 east of Huntsville.

A pleasant way to round out the day is an al fresco skate on the pond near the Muskoka Pioneer Village in Huntsville, just off Brunel Road. The pond is cleared all winter and the ice is lit up for romantic nighttime skating. Follow the sounds of the scrape of steel on ice and the happy shouts of families playing a game of shinny.

There's nothing like a day outdoors to stimulate the appetite. Unwind in front of a crackling fire and partake of the fine food at Huntsville's premier resort, Canadian Pacific's Deerhurst Inn. Deerhurst's international reputation comes from its beautiful setting — rolling hills and lakefront — extensive sporting facilities and excellent dining. The lodge dining room dates to the original 1896 Deerhurst Resort, which was the first tourist facility in the region. The menu has a Canadian emphasis, offering entrées such as loin of venison medallions, pickerel forestière, and salmon with woodland mushrooms.

Another Deerhurst eatery, Steamers, is located across the road from the main resort, and its hours vary during the winter. Enjoy the log-cabin atmosphere of Steamers during Deerhurst's maple syrup festival (mid-March to mid-April), when you can make a hearty feast of tourtière, maple smoked ham, renowned Sugar Shack chicken (with a marvellous sauce of maple syrup, chicken broth and shallots), and grand-père au sirop d'erable (a maple-flavoured dumpling). During the rest of the season, Steamers serves ample portions of Tex-Mex food.

Does the prospect of a long, grey winter have you snarling by January? The remedy is easy: pack the car and head for Huntsville.

Arrowhead Provincial Park
(705) 789-5105

Hidden Valley Highlands
(705) 789-1773

Deerhurst Resort
(705) 789-6411

34 FENELON FALLS
Jewel of the Kawarthas

Fenelon Falls and area is a good place to begin an exploration of the Kawarthas, for it is here one can find all the elements that have made the region a favourite among vacationers. Today's trip takes in a local history museum, a Trent–Severn Waterway town all dolled up for the tourist trade, and an acclaimed country inn. What are you waiting for? Grab your hat and head for the highway.

The best introduction to the Kawarthas is at the Victoria County Museum in Lindsay. The museum couldn't be easier to find. It is about 1 kilometre east of the intersection of Highways 7 and 35, at the west end of town. Household effects, pictures and text tell of the pioneer life in early Victoria County. There is also a mock-up of a nineteenth-century main street, complete with general store, pharmacy and railway station.

Travellers will head for the displays on local tourism. The Trent Canal, obsolete for commerce by the time it was completed because of improved roads and railways, soon became a boaters' paradise, and steamships and small pleasure-craft became a way of life in the region. The golden age of elegant cottaging is depicted in dioramas, photographs and journals. Consider the menu for a typical picnic: pickled tongue, cold birds, glacés, salads, jellied chicken, biscuits, lemonade.

There's more to see in Lindsay than the museum, of course. One of the main draws is the Academy Theatre, a beautifully restored facility that is home to the Kawartha Summer Theatre. The walkway linking the theatre with the downtown and with the remnants of an old mill is a popular spot on a summer day. The riverside is also the place to catch a boat cruise along the Scugog River.

Drive north from Lindsay on Highway 35 to see a small Trent Canal town that has won the hearts of travellers, Fenelon Falls. Of prime interest is the picturesque shopping area along May, Colborne and Francis Streets, where all kinds of gift, clothing and antique shops are housed in historic buildings, and the ambience is bright and cheery. The best-known stores are the Livery Stable and 20 May Street (women's clothing), Paraphernalia (gifts), Country Cupboard (gourmet foods), and Stokes-on-Trent, across the main street from most of the shops (jewellery and collector plates). Also found in the historic district is the Chatterbox Inn, which has been serving German-style cooking to shoppers for years.

The lock area is always busy, and you could easily while away the hours watching the boats, listening to the waterfall, and enjoying an ice cream from the Fenelon Falls Dairy Bar. As in Lindsay, narrated cruises depart here daily. Take a walk up Oak Street and step into an era of large mansions, gracious living, and peace and quiet. The house at the end of Oak is Maryboro Lodge, the home of James Wallis, co-founder of Fenelon Falls. Built in 1837, the Lodge now exhibits 3,500 artifacts collected over the years — among them, paintings, a grandfather clock from 1788, hair wreaths, toys, weaponry (including a bayonet and scabbard), and clothing.

Pull yourself away from the boutiques and head for Highway 121 north. At the outskirts of town, turn along County Road 25 to Sturgeon Point. Many travellers may not have heard of Sturgeon Point, but Kawartha tourism began here when a tourist resort opened in 1876. Sturgeon Point is a dignified and very private enclave of large summer homes that must be seen to be believed. It makes for a good drive or walk.

From Sturgeon Point drive north along County Road 25, make a right at County Road 8, and follow signs to Eganridge Inn and Country Club. The inn proper is a two-storey log house built in 1838 that is considered a fine example of its particular architectural style in North America. It has steep gables and a cedar roof, and a warm, honey-brown exterior. There are several guest rooms, each with reproduction furniture, whirlpool baths and other special features.

It is to the dining room, housed in the original estate barn, that most daytrippers will want to turn. Choose a table inside, near the fireplace, or venture outside on the screened balcony with its wide view of Sturgeon Lake. Lunch may be tuna-apricot-shallot salad, the much-recommended three-egg omelette, or a red pepper, ham and asparagus quiche. Dinner brings penne with steak and mushrooms, or oven-baked salmon, and tempting desserts such as profiteroles filled with ice cream on raspberry purée, or chocolate pâté with espresso and fruit sauce and fresh fruit.

Fenelon Falls calls itself the jewel of the Kawarthas. Without a doubt, it adds a certain sparkle to a gem of a day.

Victoria County Museum
May–October:
Wednesday–Sunday 1–5
(705) 324-6756

Maryboro Lodge
Mid-May–mid-June &
September–mid-October:
Saturday & Sunday 12–5
Mid-June–September:
Daily 12–5
(705) 887-1044

Eganridge Inn & Country Club
(705) 738-5111

35 KINMOUNT
Curiouser and Curiouser

There's something strange going on in the area between Fenelon Falls and Minden. This small territory that spans the boundary between the Kawarthas and Haliburton has some very uncommon sights, from the country's largest collection of movie memorabilia to one of its smallest jails. While there is no apparent explanation for this phenomenon (no reports of visiting aliens), these sights can form the basis of an unusual daytrip. To reach this mysterious region, drive north from Fenelon Falls on Highway 35.

The first town along the way is Coboconk, a good place to get out of the car for a walk. Coboconk is the site of one of Canada's smallest jails. It sits right beside the river, and has an area of roughly 5 metres by 6 metres, and limestone walls a half-metre thick. And what are the "golden years" citizens of Coboconk doing in jail? Well, they're operating Old Jail Crafts, a store stocked with home knitting and woodwork created by the senior citizens of town. It's good place to pick up a gift for those kids who don't have grandmas to knit for them.

Drive along Highway 48 west to Kirkfield. Kirkfield is well known for its hydraulic lift-lock, but before going lockside, take the time to see this quintessential small Ontario town. But what's that ahead? It looks like a Victorian mansion, all decked out with steep gables, a wraparound porch and a pretty, pale blue paint job. That's right, little Kirkfield boasts one of the Kawarthas' most renowned houses, the Sir William Mackenzie Inn.

This magnificent 40-room mansion was built in 1888 for Sir William Mackenzie, business tycoon and founding partner in the Canadian Northern Railway, the Toronto Transit Commission and Brascan, among many other concerns. This was home to Sir William and Lady Mackenzie, and was later their summer retreat. The mansion eventually fell into disrepair, but was spared an ignoble fate when Paul and Joan Scott refurbished it and opened a bed-and-breakfast establishment. The owners are pleased to give (pre-arranged) tours, and there is a small antique shop on the grounds. Occasionally there are public functions such as murder-mystery evenings in the house.

Now it is on to the famous lock. Drive north at the main (read "only") intersection on the main street to reach the lock. Lift locks are uncommon, massive structures in any setting, but the one at Kirkfield has a bizarre appearance, standing out as it does in the flat surrounding landscape. It is hard to see the canal itself below the level of the meadow grasses and flowers, so the lock appears to be an enormous grey block sitting in the middle of a field. The lock, which was built in 1907, carries boats up 15 metres in one lift.

 Head back to the car, return to Kirkfield and then east on Highway 48. Turn north at Highway 505 toward the hamlet of Victoria Road and the Museum of Temporary Art. What's that, you ask? Well, this museum, housed in the town's original general store and run by artist Michael Poulton, is devoted to baseball caps, old service-station gas pumps, and other forms of everyday art. There's nothing like it anywhere else.

Continue northbound on Highway 505 to Highway 503 and turn east. The countryside along the road is flat, with very little soil covering the limestone bedrock. This is an alvar, very uncommon in Ontario. Bird-watchers journey here in hopes of spotting a golden-winged warbler or rare loggerhead shrike.

The last and greatest sight of the day is in tiny Kinmount, so continue east along Highway 503. As you enter town, notice the sign high on the hill to the right that identifies the Highland Cinema. But this is an ordinary house, you say, are we going to watch videos in somebody's living room? But the illusion is dispelled at the entrance, for it is clear that this is no ordinary house.

Keith Stata is a movie buff, big time, and his house contains five theatres done up to look like the grand picture palaces of the golden years of cinema. The seats, box office and concession were salvaged from theatres all over Canada. The theatres, which seat from 30 to 200 people, present first-run movies every afternoon and evening all summer. You could very likely see the next blockbuster here, even before you get a chance to at home.

Even more outstanding is the collection of authentic movie posters, newspaper clippings, press releases, and photographs of all the stars. Every wall is plastered from high ceiling to floor. Several rooms are now a movie museum, with more than a hundred projectors and other movie-making equipment that date back over a century and a half. The equipment is arranged chronologically to illustrate the development of film technology, and every bit is accompanied by well-written text. The museum and posters are so intriguing that many visitors end up not even seeing a flick!

Alice in Wonderland may have seen curious sights, but the most curious a daytripper in Ontario is likely to see are those in the mysterious region straddling Haliburton and the Kawarthas.

Sir William Mackenzie Inn
(705) 438-1278

Highland Cinema
(705) 488-2107

36 HALIBURTON
A Walk on the Wild Side

Haliburton is a vast, majestic land of forested hills, lakes and rivers that sometimes plays second fiddle to its more glamorous and hectic neighbour, Muskoka. But when you are yearning for a little piece of wilderness to enjoy for its own sake, Haliburton is just the ticket.

Begin the day in the town of Minden. One of the reasons for Minden's popularity is the Kawartha Dairy. It is easy to spot: just look for the happy ice-cream customers leaving the building, and the line-up of wannabes standing on the porch. Having fed the body, you can enrich the mind at the County Town Museum and the Agnes Jamieson Gallery, located on Bobcaygeon Road just west of downtown. The former focusses on local pioneers and the latter on high-quality artwork from the local community.

Expert kayakers and canoeists are beating a track to Minden because of the quality of the Minden Whitewater Preserve on the Gull River. From town, drive north along Highway 35 to a turnoff marked Horseshoe Road 1, and follow it to the preserve. The Gull River flows through a verdant forest of hemlock and cedar, and along the river shore are lots of large boulders — good to sit on. This is a man-and-nature-made whitewater course, with massive boulders and breakwaters placed in the river to form individual rapids and frothing chutes. Most days in the summer there are groups or individuals practising their strokes through the challenging course, and neophytes may be surprised to learn that kayakers spend as much time going upstream as down. Competition days (the local tourist information office has details) provide an inspiring demonstration of athletic skill and outdoors know-how.

Head back into Minden and then east along Highway 118 to the town of Haliburton. Artists working in acrylics, watercolour, clay and fabric showcase their talents at the Rail's End Gallery, right in the centre of town. The Haliburton Highlands Museum pioneer village is found north of town along Highway 121. Its main exhibits are comprised of artifacts, tools and anecdotes from the early days of farming, railroading and lumbering; outdoors there is a log cabin, a two-storey, furnished house, a blacksmith's shop, and farm outbuildings.

Before leaving town, refuel for the next part of the day at the Old Country House Restaurant. It may be cottage country's best eatery! There are hearty servings of Roquefort steak (with homemade blue cheese), Jaegar schnitzel (with mushroom, onion and cream sauce), and a heavenly borscht. Dessert can be a melt-in-the-mouth almond meringue, white chocolate mousse cake, or a chocolate truffle raspberry cake.

From Haliburton, travel north into the hills along Highway 118, and then onto County Road 7; it's an 18-kilometre drive to the Haliburton Forest and Wild Life Reserve. There are over 8,000 hectares of forest, 50 trout lakes and 300 kilometres of mountain-bike trails open to the public, making this a large piece of heaven for those who love to camp, cottage, bike, fish, canoe, snowmobile, cross-country ski and hike.

The essential ingredient here is that the Haliburton Forest and Wild Life Reserve is privately owned and combines resource extraction (lumbering, hunting, trapping) with nature preservation — in an approach that is being studied by governments and industry around the world. It is easy to get away and be very alone on a lake, with moose, beaver and loons active around you, because the areas open to the public are at a distance from the areas under active logging. Trapping and hunting are permitted only when biking and other sports are not "in season."

The main centre of human activity is at the reserve base camp. Go to the office to pick up trail guides or to book campsites or cottages. (There are 355 campsites leased year-round, 12 for "transients," and several three-bedroom cottages with fireplaces.) The campsites have been rated the best in North America; some of them are all by themselves on a lake, other are in small groups. Base camp also provides gas and oil, a bike wash and repair shop, canoe and bike rentals, a restaurant, showers and a small grocery store.

Mountain biking is a big draw at the reserve, and whether you are a crazed daredevil keen for a test of skill and endurance, or you simply want a wooded roadway where the family can go for a spin, there is a suitable trail. Picnic sites for skiers, hikers, bikers and snowmobilers are equipped with shelters, a stove and wood. The Haliburton Forest and Wild Life Reserve has a resident wolf pack, inhabiting a 6-hectare enclosure, and by special arrangement, reserve staff lead wolf howls in late August.

Haliburton's rugged outdoors is so accessible, and yet so appealingly unspoiled, thanks to unique management activities such as those on the river in Minden and in the hills at the reserve. These two sites will tempt those who love a walk on the wild side to explore Haliburton.

County Town Museum
July & August:
Tuesday–Saturday 10–4
(705) 286-3763

Agnes Jamieson Gallery
Mid-May–mid-October:
Monday–Saturday 10–4
Mid-October–mid-May:
as above, closed Mondays
(705) 286-3763

Rail's End Gallery
January & February:
Wednesday–Saturday 10–5
March–Decenber:
Tuesday–Saturday 9–5
(705) 457-2330

Haliburton Highlands
Museum
July & August:
Daily 10–5
September–June:
Tuesday–Saturday 10–5
(705) 286-6535

Haliburton Forest and Wild
Life Reserve
(705) 754-2198

37 BUCKHORN
Art in the Rough

The natural landscape of the Kawarthas has inspired artists for decades, perhaps centuries, and the area around Buckhorn is particularly rich in studios and galleries. The internationally acclaimed Buckhorn Wildlife Art Festival held late each August draws thousands of lookers and buyers, but a visit to the region is a rewarding art trip any time of year. The following is just a wee sampling of galleries.

 A good place to plot your strategy is the Fourwinds Gallery in Selwyn (Highway 507 north of Lakefield), as the staff here can adeptly identify the best galleries to visit, according to your interest. Deceptively modest on the exterior, Fourwinds is several spacious rooms of paintings drawn from the work of local artists (owner Sue Sydney's animal portraits among them), as well as some from further afield. This is a full-service gallery, with a framing corner and a good stock of quality art supplies.

The first Kawarthan artists were those of the Ojibwa Nation of the Curve Lake Reserve on Chemong Lake. This community of 900 residents has produced many widely recognized artists, and there are several galleries on the reserve. Drive north from Fourwinds and turn west at the signpost.

Celebrated Whetung Ojibwa Crafts and Gallery, an impressive log building with a totem-pole-flanked entrance, is one of Canada's largest art showrooms. It has several floors of traditional and contemporary Native art from across the country. Paintings (originals and prints), sculpture, masks and blown glass touch on a variety of themes. Just as artful are beaded moccasins, painted paddles, and birchbark boxes decorated with traditional quill work. Next door to the gallery is a tearoom that serves corn soup, Indian bread, wild rice and buffalo burgers. Head back to Highway 507 with stops at smaller galleries such as Hannah's, Pogadakamagizowin and Wolf and Feather.

Drive along Highway 507 to Buckhorn, and then east along Highway 36 a couple of kilometres to fabulous Gallery on the Lake. If you thought the large collection at Whetung was mind-boggling, get ready for more sensory overload. Gallery on the Lake is an octagonal building several stories high tucked in among the windswept pines on the shores of Lower Buckhorn Lake. It is an attractive home for paintings in oils and watercolours, mixed-media works, sculpture in jade, soapstone and wood, Raku pottery, fabric and glass art. The number and variety of work represented is staggering; there's more diversity in artistic expression at Gallery on the Lake than in most big-city public galleries.

There are other art shops around Buckhorn. The Emerald Forest, Boat House Gallery, and Vimy Ridge Gallery are commonly recommended, so if you pass these places, do drop in. Otherwise, drive west on Highway 36 to Bobcaygeon, a town with its own healthy share of the art market. Visit Off the Wall on Canal Street in the centre of town. Much of the art in the store is guaranteed to raise a chuckle, like the terra cotta planters in the form of a wrinkled shirt or old sofa. Upstairs the atmosphere is more sedate, as suits the good collection of wildlife and landscape paintings by popular artists Bateman, Doolittle and Pong.

Ask for directions to Bobcaygeon's Public Library; its gallery of paintings from the area, the work of lesser-known and unknown artists, makes the library the very place to buy souvenir art at bargain prices. Just up the street from the library is the gallery of Karl Illini, whose work on enormous canvases emphasizes historic buildings and vintage automobiles — a change of view from the wilderness focus of the rest of the day. Three other galleries are located in town and are worth a gander: Frame of Mind and Bobcaygeon Fine Art on Bolton Street, and the Olivia Gallery north of the canal on Main Street.

It's a good idea to pick up lunch while in town. The Bobcaygeon Inn sits on the riverbank across from the downtown. Since the 1920s guests have come out to the patio to watch the boats go by; in fact, many diners arrive here by boat. The house specialty is prime rib with all the trimmings.

The last stop of the art tour may be the most enjoyable. It's the home, studio and gallery of water-colourist Chuck Burns. He has earned a wide reputation based on his sensitive depictions of rural life — kids sitting on a school bus, a Hereford gazing over a fence. Burns is often on hand (although an advance phone call is appreciated) to discuss his work and the art world in general. The Burns Gallery is close to Bobcaygeon; drive south on Highway 36 and take County Road 17 when it veers off to the left. The gallery is just along this road.

This is one of those tours where it pays to step out of the suggested route to investigate the tiny studios hidden in the woods along the backroads. The wealth of creativity and skill in the region makes it an exciting destination for anyone seeking art in the rough.

Most galleries open daily
during summer; hours vary
during winter.

Chuck Burns Gallery
(705) 738-3069

38 LAKEFIELD
Kawartha Byways

The Kawartha Lakes have an appeal that is an unparalleled blend of both natural and human elements. On today's trip, visit a site as rugged now as it was when human eyes first saw it, and call in on a couple of charming Kawartha towns, and a park that is the happy result of Mother Nature and human activity working together.

The Warsaw Caves Conservation Area should be on the agenda of any traveller to the Kawarthas. This public park is easily accessible by way of County Road 4 from Peterborough, or by Roads 32 and 4 from Lakefield. The story of the caves goes back a little ways — about 10,000 years back — to when the last glacier receded and meltwater rushed through the Indian River valley. Turbulent water entered fissures in the limestone bedrock, and eroded and dissolved the rock into subterranean caverns and channels. When boulders and loose rock were swirled about in the current, perfectly round kettles, or potholes, resulted, and these are visible throughout the park.

The Warsaw Caves Conservation Area is a hot spot for spelunkers, and is recommended for anyone with a love of adventure or in search of a cool place on a hot summer's day. Here are a few suggestions for a truly successful exploration: take along a flashlight (or buy one at the store in Warsaw); wear clothes that can get very dirty, and keep those knees covered; wear non-slip footwear.

Follow signs to the Caves Trail parking lot and from there along a short trail to seven caves, marked C1 to C7. Some of the caves are not much more than a large entranceway, while others, such as number 2, are almost 100 metres long. You can sample one or all of the caves, or even walk between some of them by way of passageways. Several of these long passages require scrambling on hands and knees. Kids love to enter by way of one cave and emerge from another, dirty from head to toe!

Cave 4 is the place to be on a hot day. It is called a glaciere cave, because the temperature remains at around 0°C year-round and ice is often found in the lower levels. Cave 4 is not for the rotund, since explorers must use a rope to rappel down a narrow, crooked incline. Cave 5 is a good choice for those who do not wish to be entirely enclosed, since this 88-metre passage is open to the sky in many places. Look up to see sinewy cedar roots actually bridging over the cave roof.

 The conservation area has other attractions. The Kettle–Lookout Trail crosses the Indian River via boardwalk, and continues up to an elevated lookout over the entire valley. There is a beach here, and canoes may be rented for a paddle on the Indian River.

Soon it is time to see a radically different side of Kawarthan beauty, the town of Lakefield. Charming is an overused adjective, but it is not wasted on Lakefield. Historic homes and public buildings abound; its citizens enjoy a rich literary tradition; and this little town is known far and wide for its ice cream. Take the time to wander through the downtown and stop at some of the book, antique and craft stores along the way.

One of Main Street's senior citizens is ivy-covered, fieldstone Christ Church Anglican, built in 1853 as a result of the efforts of Colonel Samuel Strickland. Along with sisters Susannah Moodie and Catharine Parr Traill, Strickland was part of Canada's first family of literature. (Canlit buffs can walk to the intersection of Clementi and Smith, across the river from the church, to see Traill's home.) Strickland's grave is in the church cemetery. Christ Church is undergoing renovation to restore the interior to its original appearance. The church is open in the afternoon, and it is worth a glance inside to appreciate the restful atmosphere within and to view displays that describe the history of the church.

A trip to Lakefield is not complete without a call in at Hamblin's, at Water and Bridge Streets. A dairy has stood at this corner for decades, a welcome stop for cottagers en route home. The sign on the doors reads: Through these doors pass the world's greatest ice cream eaters. The ice cream is rich and delicious, and a Hamblin's cone is perfect company for an amble north along the river. An  alternate route, River Road south toward Peterborough, is a good country drive past several small locks.

The daytrip continues westbound along Bridge Street. This route passes two more sweet attractions, Maple Corners Ice Cream (with even more flavours than Hamblin's), and the Kawartha Bakery, where homemade macaroons, doughnuts, eccles cakes, cinnamon knots and meat pies are sold hot out of the oven daily.

Head out into the countryside along County Road 18, going toward Bridgenorth. Just before entering town, take County Road 14 west across the Chemong Lake Causeway. Chemong Lake is always a cheery blue, even on overcast days. Retrace your route back over the causeway and enter the town of Bridgenorth. At the south end of town sits a century-old landmark, the Chemong Lodge, originally a cottage with a lakeside verandah and now a popular restaurant and pub. The lodge dishes up ample servings of meat-and-potato fare such as country-style ribs and steak, and Kawartha pickerel.

It is back to a southbound route along County Road 18, and then a west turn at Highway 7B. This busy highway leads to County Road 10, where signs indicate a right turn to Emily Provincial Park. Natural conditions and human activity coincide at Emily to the benefit of daytrippers and campers. The park area was once farmland that has been purchased by the Province and allowed to revert to meadow and light forest.

The expanse of marsh along Pigeon River is the main draw for outdoors-lovers, who come to walk along the Marsh Boardwalk Trail. Only 1 kilometre long, this is not an arduous trail, but it offers tremendous opportunities, such as the chance to observe an osprey both on the nest (a nesting platform maintained by park staff) and as it hovers over a fish dinner. A boardwalk allows walkers access to a cattail marsh where marsh wrens, common yellowthroat, and three species of turtle can be seen. On spring evenings the marsh comes alive with the weird sounds of American bittern and other wetland denizens. The wooded section of the trail exudes a refreshing cedar-and-fern scent; look in the trail guide to identify several uncommon plants that may be found.

An even closer look at the marshes of the river and nearby Pigeon Lake can be accomplished from the water, and there are canoe rentals at tourist outfitters just outside the park. (Ask at the park entrance for directions.) Fishermen love the river for muskie fishing, and Emily has fine beaches for the sun-and-surf crowd.

The last Kawarthan site to visit is the town of Omemee, just south of the park. Omemee is the picture of a farm country hamlet, very tiny and placid. It has several handsome older buildings, a few shops, and a micro-brewery. But the main point of a visit to town must surely be the Kawarthas' best bakery (at least on a taste-per-floor-area basis), Graham's. The bakery is small and unpretentious, and has prices that haven't changed in ages. And just dream about the delights in store: raspberry-filled neapolitans; spiced apple, nut and raisin tarts; rumballs; and fern tarts (jam, coconut, two-tone icing). The most flavourful sausage rolls in all of Ontario, meat pies, breads and salads make this the spot to pick up a good-sized snack for the trip home.

Today's tour of some of Kawartha's parks and villages is a combination of outdoor beauty and human cultivation that will win you back to Kawartha's byways time and time again.

Warsaw Caves
Conservation Area
Mid-May–July &
September–mid-October:
Weekends 9–5
July & August:
Daily 9–9
(705) 745-5791

Emily Provincial Park
Late May–mid-October:
Daily 8 AM–10 PM
(705) 799-5170

Chemong Lodge
(705) 292-8435

39 ALGONQUIN PROVINCIAL PARK
A Tale of Two Parks

The name "Algonquin" sends a shiver down the spine of any Ontarian with a passion for the outdoors. Even those who have never visited the park associate the name with images of the wild: a moose standing deep among the lily pads, water dripping from its raised head; a wide-angle view of crimson maples on hills that stretch to the horizon; a lone paddler shrouded in mist. Although hikers and canoeists rejoice in 7,700 square kilometres of backcountry wilderness, there is a second Algonquin, a ribbon of easily accessible lands along Highway 60, that is tailor-made for those who seek a briefer — and less demanding — taste of Algonquin's magic appeal.

Algonquin Park staff are justifiably proud of the visitor centre, which opened to commemorate the park's centenary in 1993. (The visitor centre is at Kilometre 43, which means it is 43 kilometres east along Highway 60 from the park's west gate.) A centre tour properly begins with the superb narrated slide-presentation in the theatre. It provides a dramatic overview of the park's history from the time when the rocks of the Canadian Shield were warped and moulded, through the first visits by aboriginal people about 5,000 years ago, to the devastation wreaked in modern times by logging and fire. What took nature one billion years and four ice ages to create took man less than one lifetime to modify forever. Visitors exit the movie theatre onto a balcony high over the forest; far below, orange and red canoes thread their way through a wetland, and all on the balcony feel the itch to join the adventure.

The centre's excellent reputation is owed in large measure to its exhibits, especially the dioramas, which make viewers feel that they have entered the private world of moose, bear and beaver. Artist Dwayne Harty has made his mark as an expert with these three-dimensional mock-ups of scenes such as an owl and ravens at a winter kill, or a forest scene in which deer, ruffed grouse, a least flycatcher and Algonquin's ever-present deer mouse take their natural places among Indian pipes, Dutchman's-breeches and red trillium. The display at which travellers pause the longest is the underwater world; this unique point of view stops at the underside of the surface, and all that we see is what is in the lake. A school of minnows flashes, a fish approaches a lure, the head, belly and feet of a loon break the surface.

The centre includes some cleverly designed computer games, such as the reproduction game, or spruce bog roulette. In this roulette game, players guess at the life expectancy of bog inhabitants such as spruce grouse or the leatherleaf plant. You will be more successful than most players if you know in advance that fewer than two percent of all Algonquin inhabitants reach their life expectancy, and most live only a few days.

 Human history in Algonquin is short, but intense, and there are many displays of text, maps and historic photographs of the logging era, railroads and summer camps. The most surprising exhibits describe summertime at the 13 hotels and resorts that were built in the early years of this century. One such resort was the luxurious Highland Inn, which had a hundred rooms, a formal dining room, a tennis court, dance pavilion, marina and train station. (Three lodges exist in the park to this day — Arowhon Pines, Killarney Lodge and Bartlett's — and they welcome those with reservations to their dining rooms.) Children like to spend time listening to Emiel the logger (an animated model) tell of his life in the woods. They also enjoy a visit to the fire-tower cabin to find out how forest-fire watchers did their job.

The Friends of Algonquin operate a gift shop with a broad selection of guide books, recordings, clothing and Algonquin memorabilia. The centre also has a cafeteria with snacks and full meals.

Fully equipped with advice from the staff, head for the out-of-doors. Everyone should take in at least one day-hike. The Highway 60 corridor has 13 day-trails that range from 0.8 kilometres to

11 kilometres in length. Park staff can provide trail guides and a description of each trail. The longest day-trail, Mizzy Lake, is also the most recommended (water-resistant footwear is a good idea). Its 11 kilometres of hiking and nine lakes offer the best chance of seeing Algonquin's famous animals; in spring and fall, visitors will almost be sure to see beaver, moose, broadwinged hawks, painted turtles and loons. Especially keen wildlife-watchers will want to check out the sightings board in the visitor centre before heading out. Travellers unable to hike should consult with staff about the best places along the highway to see animals. Early morning and evening are, as everywhere, the best times for wildlife viewing.

 The Spruce Bog Boardwalk (1.5 kilometres) is the trail nearest the visitor centre; its booklet explains important features of bog ecology. Steeply ascending Lookout Trail (1.9 kilometres) and Booth's Rock Trail (5.1 kilometres) lead to observation points over hundreds of square kilometres of forested hills. They are beautiful in any season, but stunning in autumn when every view is fully saturated with orange and crimson. Visitors may choose their trail according to their interest; trail guides cover topics as diverse as river ecology, park geology and railroad history.

Mountain bikers now have their own trail in Algonquin. Minnesing Trail is moderately difficult; it has four loops that total 23.4 kilometres in length. There are plans to add a family-style bike trail for the summer of 1996. It will be 10 kilometres in length and travel sections of an old railbed.

Folk who love to be near water can also have a great day along the Highway 60 corridor. Small-mouth bass, lake trout, brook trout and splake can be found in many lakes; the spring fishing is especially good. There's swimming on several lakes, and sandy beaches on Lake of Two Rivers. Waterside picnic sites abound throughout the Highway 60 corridor, and the attractive site at the Tea Lake Dam is also a good spot to swim in the river. Canoe enthusiasts will want to head for the

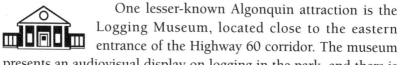

Portage Store on Canoe Lake. The store supplies equipment and advice on good locations for a day-canoe — one of the best being Canoe Lake itself (two to three hours) — and will transport a canoe to anywhere in the corridor. Guided day-long canoe trips can also be reserved.

Park staff run a full schedule of nature-oriented activities such as guided walks, evening slide shows and lectures, children's programs, canoe outings, and canoe and camping demonstrations. Sensational August and September wolf howls take place on Thursday evenings beginning at around 9 PM. Guides take visitors (usually as many as a thousand in number) to a previously identified wolf "rendezvous" site. Wolves may be enticed into answering the imitation howls given by the naturalist. These special moments are peak, often spine-tingling, experiences in the life of any nature lover. As with any animal adventure, success is never a sure thing, but the track record of Algonquin staff is good: wolves have responded on 20 of the last 22 howls.

One lesser-known Algonquin attraction is the Logging Museum, located close to the eastern entrance of the Highway 60 corridor. The museum presents an audiovisual display on logging in the park, and there is a 1-kilometre interpretive trail with exhibits of logging equipment, a camboose shanty where over 50 loggers slept and ate during the winter logging season, and a blacksmith shop (needed because horses were active in the logging industry here until the 1950s).

The last word on the wonders of Algonquin must be that this is a true four-season destination. Snowshoeing and cross-country skiing conditions are excellent in the Highway 60 corridor. In the backcountry, once the visitors of summer have disappeared, you share the park with only the gray jays and wolves.

Algonquin is truly two parks in one. A daytrip to the visitor centre and trails in the Highway 60 corridor can be enjoyed on its own merits, and could prove an enticing lure to a longer sojourn in the wilderness of the "other" Algonquin.

Algonquin Provincial Park
Visitor Centre
Late April–November:
Daily, varying hours

Logging Museum
Mid-May–mid-October:
Daily 10–6
(613) 637-2828

Portage Store
(613) 633-5622

40 BEWDLEY
Rice Lake Tour

Visitors have been enjoying Rice Lake's scenery and bountiful fishery for thousands of years, ever since early hunting and gathering tribes came here for the pickerel and the deer. The Rice Lake of today continues to lure travellers keen for outdoor recreation and a fine country inn.

 Lovely countryside scenery begins even before you reach Rice Lake, which is why the suggested route is to leave Highway 401 at exit 448 (Newtonville), travel north to County Road 9, and from there east toward Rice Lake. The picture through the windscreen is every daytripper's dream: a ribbon of asphalt rising and falling over long, steep hills, neat red barns beside white farmhouses, and small crossroads villages. Quaint Garden Hill is one such village, its tiny general store and millpond nostalgic reminders of the time when this community boasted eight mills on the river.

Bewdley calls itself a gateway to Rice Lake; the eye-catching sign at the turnoff from County Road 9 is impossible to miss. The road curves into town between tall white pines, and just beyond the last turn, there it is, Rice Lake, set into a green-and-gold checkerboard of fields, its surface speckled with bobbing boats. This is serious fishing territory, and Bewdley makes a good living as caterer to the throngs who arrive annually to match wits with pickerel, bass and pike, and that shark of the Kawarthas, giant muskie. Rice Lake has produced huge fish harvests every year for eons, and it continues to provide a catch of over 11,000 kilograms annually. Try your luck with the crowd at the dock, or rent a boat and tackle from any one of the marinas in town.

Rice Lake is long and narrow, so that from Bewdley it stretches east-west 30 kilometres away to the horizon, although it is only 5 kilometres across. At one time it was filled with wild rice, a staple food for Native peoples and settlers alike, but the construction of the Trent Canal flooded the shallow rice-growing areas, and the crop was eliminated.

Return to County Road 9 and drive east to County Road 18, where a northward turn leads to the village of Gore's Landing. There is no sign of steamboats today, but in the 1830s Gore's Landing owed its existence to the boats that picked up stagecoach passengers from Port Hope and carried them to Peterborough. For about 50 years Gore's Landing has been summer home to well-heeled Torontonians, whose white clapboard retreats stand on the hill near the shore.

 At the intersection in town (at the general store), turn east and follow the road to the Victoria Inn. What a joy for a road-weary traveller to come upon this three-storey estate home, with its distinctive cedar shakes, stained glass, and manicured lawns. Victoria Inn has an interesting past. It was built in 1902 as The Willows, a summer retreat and studio for Gerald S. Hayward, painter of miniature portraits. The miniatures were painted on ivory, and were treasured in the days before photography. His clients included Edward VII, the czar and czarina of Russia, presidents and prime ministers.

The dining room is in an enclosed porch along the lake side of the building. The kitchen specializes in fresh country cuisine: spinach-basil soup or trout chowder are followed by a sandwich or grilled chicken at lunch, and pasta, steak or pine-baked trout at dinner. Cheesecake, fresh fruit pies and chocolate mousse cake round out any meal. Victoria Inn's hospitality and fine food will have most travellers promising to return sometime for a weekend in one of the inn's ten rooms, each of which has either a lake view or a fireplace.

County Road 18 continues east to Harwood. There you can make a stop at the Harwood Fish Culture Station and find out how fish are raised for release into the lake. Harwood also has a couple of craft and gift shops for pleasant browsing. Just east of Harwood is a small picnic stop, the Alnwick Conservation Area. In fact, due to the paucity of public lands around the lake, this is the only really good place along the southern shore for seeing the water from a height. Alnwick does not disappoint, however, for from here you can see the entire length of the lake and its many islands. Some of these landforms are not much more than shallow spots where willows appear to magically float on the water, and others are curious, hump-backed formations covered in forest. The latter are actually drumlins, gravelly hills formed during the last ice age, and drumlins are what you have driven up and down all along Road 18. The journey can end here, or you can continue to the eastern tip of the lake and Hastings, where there are shops and restaurants to explore.

Thousands of travellers agree that Rice Lake is the place to visit for scenery, country hospitality and outdoor activity. And in this case at least, the crowd is right.

Victoria Inn
(905) 342-3261

41 KEENE
A Keene Sense of History

The area around Keene, on the north shore of Rice Lake, is one of those rare locales where many different facets of Ontario's history can be appreciated in one day. From the ancient burial sites at Serpent Mounds to the up-to-date facilities at Elmhirst's Resort, so much of our past is alive and well in Keene.

The day starts at a site that is truly ancient by Ontario standards. Exit the 401 at Highway 28 north, turn east at County Road 2 and follow it to Keene. Signs point the way south to Rice Lake and Serpent Mounds Provincial Park.

Serpent Mounds has been set apart to ensure the protection of burial mounds used by the early Point Peninsula people. The activity centre presents the history of this site, gleaned through archaeological digs of the mounds themselves as well as "middens," or garbage heaps.

Nomadic people visited here every spring or summer from approximately 2,000 to 1,600 years ago in order to bury their dead and to live off the richness of Rice Lake. Their diet consisted largely of deer, turtle, clams and wild rice. Turtle shell was also used in pottery making. Far from being an isolated nomadic group, the people who travelled to Rice Lake were active in a trade network covering much of North America, as evidenced by finds of copper (Lake Superior), silver (Ottawa Valley), and conch (Mexico).

After the visitor centre, head just outside the door to begin the short but steep pathway to the burial mounds themselves. On top of the hill there are eight oval mounds and one large, sinuous one. Perhaps the special atmosphere at the hill comes from to the fact that you stand on sacred ground and that ancient people are buried right here under these mounds, or perhaps it is because at one time they also stood at this vantage point and admired the same view of island-dotted Rice Lake.

Since we've looked Rice Lake through the eyes of very early visitors, it's time to see what some fortunate contemporary travellers enjoy. Drive back to Highway 2 and then east to Elmhirst's Resort. The Elmhirst family has lived on this property for over a century, and four generations of the family live and work here to this day. The result is a genteel family resort with a full slate of amenities — there's even a private airstrip for guests. The elegant dining room is blessed with a wide-angle view of the lake, and is a good place for lunch or Sunday brunch. The noon menu ranges from scallop roll to beef teriyaki for the main courses, and includes cappuccino soufflé, Black Forest cake and local fruit pies for dessert.

After Elmhirst's, return to the village of Keene. This quiet rural town has spruced itself up for the tourist trade and has several stores, among them Outdoor Images, Cactus Corner and Patricia's Victorian Treasures. The main intersection has a tearoom, and kitty corner, a lunch counter; both places offer delectable home baking.

The last segment of the day, Lang Pioneer Village, is a doorway to yet another part of Ontario's history. Lang has quickly moved into the ranks of top-drawing villages, and rightly so, for its large cadre of volunteers are hospitable, knowledgeable and dedicated.

Lang comprises 18 buildings, representing many elements of a nineteenth-century Ontario settlement. Homes include cramped and primitive Fife cabin (restored to 1825) and Milburn House (restored to 1877); a wood stove, indoor pump and wallpaper were amenities enjoyed only by established farm families. Village businesses include the Keene Hotel, where, for a dime, a traveller could "flop" for the night on a wooden floor and straw tick, and the general store, which sells Lang-made tin cookie-cutters, candles and homespun yarn. The pièce-de-résistance is a handsome stone gristmill, Lang Mill. Built in 1846, the mill was updated after a fire in 1896, and continues to produce flour to this day.

Lang is a living, working village, and costumed interpreters in every building pause to chat as they practise old-time hymns on the church pump-organ, dye yarn over a front-yard fire, pound on an anvil in the blacksmith shop, or turn out a political poster on a flat-bed press. Few pioneer villages offer the active visitor program that Lang does; there are days to celebrate sheep and wool, pioneer contests, canoes, gardens and autumn harvest. Every special-event day has fun activities and — Lang staff love to pamper their guests — an abundance of food, from freshly made cider to strawberry shortcake. Lang reopens at Christmas for horse and sleigh rides, music, and yes, more food.

There are not many places in the province where you can survey almost 2,000 years of our history in one day. This trip makes it so enjoyable, you'll be sure to pick up a Keen(e) sense of history.

Serpent Mounds Provincial Park
Mid-May–September:
8 AM–10 PM
(705) 295-6879

Elmhirst's Inn
(705) 295-4591

Lang Pioneer Village
Mid-May–mid-October:
Monday–Friday 11–5
Sunday 1–6
Saturday & Holidays 1–5
(705) 295-6694

42 GRAFTON
Time Is on Our Side

Travelling country backroads in search of that elusive old Ontario chest, Depression glassware, or fashionable folk art has become a passion for many Ontarians. Northumberland County, which begins at Lake Ontario's shore and reaches north to Rice Lake, is prime antique-hunting territory. It is far enough away from Toronto to ensure reasonable prices, and Northumberland's unspoiled countryside forms the perfect setting for a day's outing.

Start the day in Grafton (take 401 exit 437 south-bound). Many people are unaware of this village, one of the most captivating in Southern Ontario. Part of its charm lies in its exceptionally well-preserved historic homes and public buildings and part lies in the fact that there are three (count em, three) quality antique shops around town.

At the corner of Highway 2 and Danforth Road is a fine neo-classical commercial building, an appropriate home for 1812 Antiques. There are many fine English items here, such as a Regency maple and mahogany table, a brass Victorian shoe display-stand, and a Wedgwood Irish whiskey key. In the same building are housed the Tole Lantern, with its dozens of novel lamps and shades (from tin to silk), and St. John's Books, an excellent source for children's and adults books.

1812 Antiques is also the place to ask for a highly recommended walking-tour booklet describing buildings of note in Grafton. Much of Grafton is very old by Ontario standards, and reflects the love of Georgian and Regency architecture of the United Empire Loyalists who settled here in the province's early years. Since very little has been marred or altered in a century and a half, a walk through town is like stepping into the past.

From the centre of town, drive west along Highway 2. Just outside of Grafton are two must-sees, Van Schyndel–Lachapelle Antiques and Spaulding's. Van Schyndel's will weaken the knees of any folk-art lover. Two floors in a renovated barn display unequalled work from Quebec, the Ottawa Valley and the Maritimes: wooden farm animals, decorated window-benches, carved pieces for over windows, and cupboards. All pieces sport a complete description, original paint, and a impressive price tag.

 Spaulding's, next door, is a 180-degree about-face in atmosphere. This large home has several rooms of china, silver and glassware, as well as large pieces such as an 1838 pianoforte and an 1850 rosewood melodeon. Few people will be able to pass by the plentiful display of antique jewellery in brass, silver and ivory without purchasing at least one special piece.

Continue to drive west from Grafton, stopping at the Barnum House Museum, an impressive white home built in 1819 for successful farmer, mill-owner and publican Eliakim Barnum. Items of interest pointed out by costumed interpreters include mirrored sconces, a hurricane lamp, a "magic lantern" (precursor of the stereoscope), clavichord and dulcimer. A description of the architectural features provides a history lesson along the way. The cross-and-Bible design carved on the front door indicated to passers-by that this house was occupied by devout Anglicans. The unusual shelflike nook near the ceiling behind the kitchen fireplace is called a granny seat, and is where the senior member of the family slept on cold nights. Barnum House staff serve afternoon tea and home baking in the sedate ballroom.

After Barnum House, it is back to the antique trail. Return to Grafton and drive north on Lyle  Street toward the 401, but pass over the highway into the rolling, pastoral countryside. Northumberland is still family-farm country, with uninterrupted views all around of crops and pasture, immaculate homes and barns. The hills provide a great panorama to the south of sparkling Lake Ontario, so stop the car to better appreciate the scenery before driving on.

At the intersection with County Road 22 there is a choice to be made. You can head east toward Morganstown to investigate the large display of glassware at Ray Cobbing Antiques. Many pieces date to the 1930s and carry names such as American sweetheart, cornflower and princess. Cobbing's is unusual among antique shops in that its glassware is often available in full sets. Alternatively, drive west to Highway 45 and then south to Baltimore and Red Kettle Antiques (located on Highway 45 just south of town). The Kettle stocks an eclectic supply of Canadiana — irons and trivets, oil lamps and church pews, as well as Delft china, Japanese Occupation china, and more. Head west off Baltimore's main drag to see the 150-year-old mill, painted with signs that advertise pastry flour and "cash-for-wheat."

Squeeze into the car, settle the wooden cow beside the candlebox, double-check on the carefully wrapped punch bowl on the back seat, and jingle those funky Victorian bracelets. All set? Then it's homeward bound.

Barnum House Museum
Late May–September:
Thursday–Monday 10–5
(905) 349-2656

43 PETERBOROUGH
Pride and Joy

Peterborough is the best city in the province to live in — just ask anyone born and raised here. Civic pride runs deep, and rightly so, for Peterborough boasts beautiful natural surroundings, an interesting past and a vibrant commercial core.

Civic duty and pride runs not only deep, but long as well. In 1836, Peterborough residents could not stand the thought of losing their beloved Doctor Hutchison to a more lucrative position in Toronto, so volunteers built him a lovely, two-storey brick home at 270 Brock Street as an enticement for him to remain. The house was home, office, surgery and dental clinic, and its doors are again open to the public, but this time as a museum that recreates both the domestic and working life of a busy doctor at a time when house calls were made on horseback and doctors were paid in chickens or bearskin rugs.

Hutchison's office is furnished to period with medical instruments, a doctor's carpet bag, cash box, pharmaceutical equipment, and a tiny chair for examining children. A parlour, bedrooms, and a basement keeping-room are also authentically furnished, and costumed guides provide tours. Sandford Fleming (later Sir Sandford), the great surveyor and engineer, designer of Canada's beaver postage-stamp and creator of Standard Time, was a cousin of Hutchison's, and lived in this house while he surveyed the region. His room contains early lithographs and maps, antique surveyor's tools, and clothing, and there are jottings from his journal for various inventions, including what looks like a prototype for inline skates.

Hutchison House has a basement gift shop, and there is a period herb garden on the grounds. Scottish teas are served on summer afternoons, and you should check the schedule for other special events planned with the entire

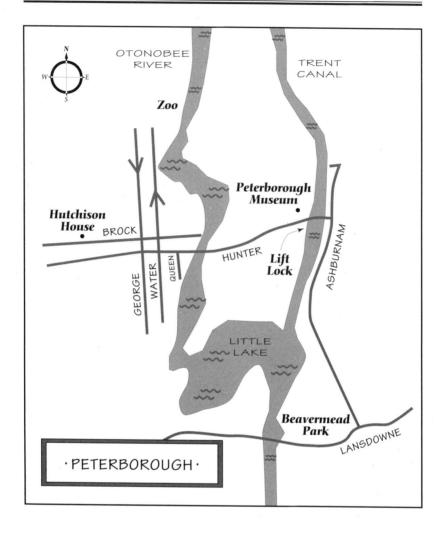

family in mind. The surrounding neighbourhood is a quiet, shaded walk, and a walking-tour guide is available at Hutchison House.

Peterborough's most famous symbol is the lock on the Trent Canal. Typical of a town that thinks big things of itself, this gargantuan concrete construction is the world's tallest hydraulic lift-lock. Models and slide shows in the activity centre (just off Hunter Street) provide thorough explanations on the workings of

the lock that non-technical people can readily under-
stand. Upon its completion in 1904, the lock was a
unique source not only of local but of national pride;
it was described as a "victory over mud, bad weather and technical
problems." At the visitor centre you can sit in a model of a small
boat, and a film will provide a nerve-racking sense of what a trip
through the lock is like, as your vessel is raised 20 metres straight
into the air, with nothing but a deceptively thin-looking gate
between you and open space. Step outside the centre onto a balcony to observe the lock in operation.

Once you've had your fill of watching boats go through the
lock, return to Hunter Street and turn left, as if driving back to
downtown, but make a left at Queen Street and find Charlotte
Anne's restaurant. Just when Ontario heat and humidity has worn
you down, cheer up with Charlotte Anne's tingling frozen fruit
cocktails (alcoholic and non-), which can be enjoyed inside on
recycled church pews, or better yet, out back on the quiet walled
patio. The menu includes uncommonly good salads, lasagna,
sandwiches (a terrific Reuben), chicken with brandy cream, beef
stir-fry, and calorie-laden desserts such as caramel brownie cheesecake. One could spend an entire afternoon here, but there's more
of Peterborough to see.

Drive along Hunter back to the lift lock, this time
passing right underneath it; turn right at Ashburnham
for a pleasant drive along the canal to what many residents love most about their pretty city, Peterborough's pride and
joy, Little Lake. Along its eastern shore (the one nearest you) is
Beavermead Park, with hundreds of camp sites conveniently close
to downtown yet with a waterfront view, picnic sites, minigolf,
walking trails and playing fields. At one end of Beavermead is a
public garden that demonstrates environmentally
sound methods of landscaping and gardening. There
are special talks and exhibits here all summer long.

Little Lake is also the place to catch the tour boat that sails
through the lift lock and up the canal past the modern campus of
Trent University. After dark, the fountain in the middle of Little

Lake is lit by coloured floodlights. The Festival of Lights, an outdoor stage show, takes place Wednesday and Saturday evenings in Creary Park on the shores of Little Lake.

Peterborough's confidence and sparkle are contagious, and a visit to the city is bound to have you in agreement with residents who are mighty pleased to live here.

Hutchison House
May–December:
Tuesday–Sunday 1–5
January–March:
Monday–Friday 1–5
(705) 743-9710

Peterborough Lift Lock Activity Centre
Mid-May–mid-October:
Daily 10–5
(705) 742-2251

44 PETERBOROUGH
Slip-Slidin' Away

I t's been said, and truly, that there are no feet in Canada during the winter. Look around at those who enjoy life outdoors — there are blades, runners, and skis, but few plain feet — which leads to the conclusion that the best way to cope with winter is to snap on your favourite footgear and head out for some fresh-air fun.

Peterborough is a prime location for wintertime escapades, as it has superior sites for several sports located within a small area. Once in town, follow directional signs to the Trent Canal and Peterborough's hydraulic lift-lock. The blue waters of summer have been transformed into a thick layer of smooth natural ice, a delight for skaters and hockey players who enjoy this fabulous outdoor rink as long as weather permits, usually from the first of January to March. There are separate sections for recreational skating and hockey (goalposts provided), so all can enjoy the canal at their own pace. The canal is uncrowded — on a weekday you may have the place to yourself — and you can get up a good speed along the half-kilometre route. Skaters pass under iron bridges and alongside trees that in summer provided shade for boaters and now shelter wintering crows.

Skate till your legs call for a rest and then drive west on Hunter Street (which is the street crossing over the canal and lock) and follow the signs right up the hill to the Peterborough Centennial Museum and Archives. The parking lot here serves two attractions, the museum and a terrific toboggan hill. First, head for the toboggan hill, which is just east of the parking lot, behind the museum. The hill is steep, long, uncrowded, and just the thing for

family fun. It runs through treed parkland, and is slightly banked at the sides for easy steering. After a few good runs you'll be ready to head to the museum to warm up indoors.

The Peterborough Centennial Museum takes the visitor on a polished trip through regional history, beginning with the glacial eskers and moraine, through to the earliest inhabitants, the Mississauga, to the explorations of Champlain to the twentieth century. The days of pioneering farmers and early commerce are illustrated with an abundance of photographs, maps, documents and informative text, and attractive displays of split-rail fences, farm and domestic tools and clothing. The vast differences between the lives of the landed gentry and those of Irish peasant farmers is described, as are early sawmills, railways, churches, schools and political life.

The museum's changing exhibits cover topics such as woodworking, architectural heritage, and the work of local photographers. Special events are staged throughout the year, and the museum gift shop sells books and gift items with a historical theme.

If your feet and face have warmed up, it's time to head outdoors again. Drive along Hunter Street to Water Street. Turn right (north) and follow the river to Riverview Park and Zoo. A wintertime zoo trip may be unconventional, but is the only time to learn how animals cope with snow and freezing temperatures. Kids go wild with excitement over the extensive adventure playground, since in the off-season they have it as their own exclusive domain. The zoo occupies about 20 hectares of parkland on a hilltop overlooking the Otonabee River, and is home to dozens of animals, including cougar, yak and llama. Notice the totem pole, one of the tallest in Canada. Drive along the Otonabee River north of the zoo; the rapids here attract several kinds of overwintering ducks, such as bufflehead and merganser.

For some people, the main point of winter in the great outdoors is the pleasure of thawing out over a cup of steaming hot chocolate. Peterborough, already the envy of the region for its winter facilities, has not one but two tempting spots for refreshments. Haaselton's is on George Street, downtown; right around the corner is Fancies on Hunter Street.

Haaselton's is the place for designer warm-ups, with over ten kinds of espresso and three kinds of hot chocolate. Haaselton's bear tummy warmer, for example, is steamed milk, frothy milk and strawberry syrup. You can pick from chocolate eclairs and a medley of muffins and cakes to accompany your drinks. Fancies is also rewarding for the ice-and-snow set, with ample breakfasts starting very early in the day. Their famous muffins and cinnamon buns are made on the premises, as are premium desserts and cream teas.

When the land lies deep in new snow and icicles tinkle in the trees, it's time to visit Peterborough, a city where it is a treat to be slip-slidin' away.

Peterborough Centennial Museum and Archives
Mid-May–mid-October:
Monday–Friday 12–5
Saturday & Sunday 12–5
Mid-October–mid-May:
Daily 10–5
(705) 743-5180

45 PORT HOPE
Antique Mystique

Port Hope is an antique-hunter's dream, with over a dozen shops within walking distance of one another. Not only is the shopping inspiring; it is enchanting too, as it takes place in a town that has effectively held the worst of the twentieth century at bay. Port Hope's downtown of well-preserved nineteenth-century buildings set along the steep slope of the Ganaraska River valley glows with small-town charm.

The exploration begins on Walton Street (the main street of town), near the top of the hill, at the Owl & the Pussycat. The antique shop here specializes in Canadian butter boxes, harvest tables and locally produced pottery; the adjacent tearoom serves scones, sandwiches and a variety of teas on a patio overlooking downtown Port Hope.

Start the descent down Walton Street. Drop into Linton Shaw Gallery if your interest extends to contemporary art in jewellery, paintings, col- lage or glass. More art for the home can be found across the street at Lord Russborough's Annex, which is filled with European and Canadian prints, maps and paintings that date to the eighteenth century. Expert staff will help you locate a map or print that pertains to your locale or ancestry. The same shop sells restored and Tiffany lamps and stained-glass panels.

If visiting Lord Russborough's Annex is like entering the parlour of your wealthy great-aunt, then a trip to Chatwood & Simmons is like stepping into her dining room. There's plenty here for lovers of Victorian china, sterling and table linens. Anyone would be delighted by the miniature sterling pincushions and by the antique jewellery in silver, amethyst and amber.

Cross the street and head to three-storey, redbrick Smith's Creek Antiques. The many fine items in this huge store encompass popular culture over the centuries. Occasional items include rocking horses, paintings, and an extraordinary travelling tea-set, with a fine china tea-service nestled in a rugged suitcase. As you walk back up the hill, you can make short detours along Queen and John Streets.

Number 12 Queen Street houses Estate Treasures, Lee Caswell Antiques, and Simmons & Whitmore Antiques (the latter two are on the third floor, by appointment only). It would take several dozen large buffets to hold all the silverware and china at Estate Treasures, some of it antique and some second-hand; there are also small furnishings such as tables and lamps.

John Street is the location of Discovery House, with its original artwork, mainly paintings, and some furniture and folk art. The same narrow hallway leads to Picker's Market, which offers typical flea-market items as well as antiques; it's a good choice for bargain hunters.

Return to Walton Street and locate Antique Associates, actually three dealers under one large roof. This is prime hunting-ground, stocked with many unique items you won't find elsewhere. Be on the lookout for century-old map tubes, a wonderful nut-roasting/vending machine, a muffin table of mahogany with satinwood inlay.

 You may want to reminisce about the antique delights encountered thus far over lunch. John Street has two historically correct dining places. On the corner of Augusta there's the Carlyle Inn, an elegant Italianate building that began life as a branch of the Bank of Upper Canada (1857). The foyer and dining room have high ceilings, plaster mouldings and luxurious decoration. Plane Crazy, the Carlyle's pub, is a whimsical eatery with a vintage aircraft motif. The Carlyle's menu has something for everyone, from bratwurst to pork bordelaise.

Just down the street is the Beamish Pub, specializing in hearty British pub food. It was built in 1848 as the home and shop of Port Hope's first shoemaker. Interestingly, this building has been moved twice in its lifetime, although it has always remained on John Street.

After lunch there are more antique shops to explore. Just ask any merchant for the brochure with details on locations. If you wish to investigate Port Hope's historic neighbourhoods, then head for Mill and King Streets on the east side of the Ganaraska River. The Canadian Fire Fighters Museum is located at 95 Mill Street; this institution chronicles firefighting through displays, photographs and special events. Exhibits include eight firefighting rigs, horse-drawn, hand-drawn and contemporary, from the period 1830 to 1955.

Stroll along King Street, a showcase of nineteenth-century homes of the well-to-do. Bluestone, on the corner of Dorset, catches the eye of every passerby. When it was built in 1834, Bluestone was an architectural triumph, with its regal blend of Georgian symmetry and Greek revival details, and is today considered one of the most beautifully restored early homes in the province. Beloved St. Mark's Anglican Church is at 51 King Street. This frame church with the tall steeple has a quaint cemetery that is the burial place of Governor General Vincent Massey.

Bid adieu to the hustle and hassle of big-city antique-hunting and visit quiet Port Hope. You'll come away with real finds at good prices, and memories of a well-preserved town.

Canadian Fire Fighters Museum
Mid-June–September:
Daily 10–5
(705) 885-8337

46 MOUNT JULIAN
Stoney Lake Then and Now

Stoney Lake, the largest, easternmost and least settled of the Kawartha Lakes, isn't just for cottagers: a tour along the lake's northern shore is an enjoyable daytrip that combines historic sites and refreshing lake scenery.

Stoney Lake has been a visiting place for many since early times, when Native carvers left their mark by way of petroglyphs, or rock carvings. Petroglyphs Provincial Park, at the eastern end of the lake, was created to protect of the highest concentration of such carvings in Canada. Take Highway 28 east, and follow directional signs along a gravel road to Petroglyphs. The petroglyphs are a 10-to-15-minute walk from the parking lot, although there is a closer lot for those with mobility difficulties.

A large, rounded outcrop of white marble is etched with hundreds of figures, large and small, thought to be the work of Algonkian people between 500 and 1,000 years ago. Many of the carvings are very black and well defined, while others are faint and imprecise. To prevent further loss due to weathering, a specially designed glass-and-steel building was constructed around the outcrop. The precise meaning of the human and animal forms has been lost forever, although the images themselves — turtles, snakes, spirit boats, and large figures thought to be the creator, Gitche Manitou — are clearly significant spiritually.

There may be several reasons why this particular rock was chosen for carving, such as its underground streams and springs, but the site continues today to be revered among native spiritual leaders, as evidenced by the ceremonial sites seen on the rock. Every visitor comes away touched by the spell of the hushed, reverential atmosphere of Petroglyphs.

Leave the park, return to Highway 28 and drive west. Head for Mount Julian–Viamede, the home of Stoney Lake boat cruises.

The cruises carry passengers on a two-hour trip among Stoney's 1,100 islands. Most of the islands have cottages on them that were built in the early years of the century; with their white frame exterior, green shingles and stone chimneys, they epitomize Canadian summers well spent.

The cruise captain recounts wonderful stories of Stoney Lake cottages, their owners, and life on the lake during the elegant steamboat era. Families, servants included, travelled by train from Union Station in Toronto to Lakefield, and then on to the cottage by steamboat. Notice that cottage docks still sport the heavy iron rings used to moor steamboats; the flagpoles seen at so many of the islands were used to signal passing steamers that someone at the cottage wanted to be picked up. The buildings right at the water's edge were not originally actually cottages, but are renovated boathouses and servants' quarters from "the good old days."

The most lively reminder of Stoney Lake's grand years is the residents' recreation club and dance pavilion. The canoeing, tennis and sailing lessons offered by the association are popular to this day, and your cruise will pass by a large fleet of small sailboats bobbing and tilting. The cottagers have their own church, St. Peter's Church on the Rock, which appears rather cottagelike itself. The boats of guests are tied up at the wharf two and three deep for church weddings. The captain will also recount the history of Stoney's quarrying days, when the granite of Eagle Mount Island was cut up and slid onto barges for a long trip to Ottawa, where it became part of our Parliament Buildings.

Stoney Lake has several summer retreats worthy of special mention. There's the Bridge, a cantilevered glass building with underground passages to two boathouses and a biplane dock; it was the setting for a couple of episodes of *All My Children*. "Rompin'" Ronnie Hawkins's cottage, with its state-of-the-art recording studio, is also pointed out. It took imported Scots stonemasons three years to build Davis Island Manor, a wedding gift for the daughter of Senator George Cox. The cottage had a 460-

square-metre living room, and a stone watertower 18 metres high supplied every room with hot and cold water.

The boat returns to the dock at the Mt. Julian Hotel, the oldest resort in the Kawarthas, built in 1874. Covering the back wall of the hotel bar are 44 paintings by local resident Captain Clague, who worked on them between 1874 and 1876. They depict people, animals and other scenes from his many ocean voyages.

Next door to the Mt. Julian Hotel is the Viamede Resort. It was constructed in 1903, and has since been completely modernized, with facilities for volleyball, waterskiing, jet-skiing, exercise and riding. The dining room has a panoramic view of water and islands, and has a reputation as the place to dine in the area, especially for Sunday brunch. Lunchtime fare includes burgers, salads and sandwiches, but dinnertime brings escargots, chateaubriand and pork Wellington to cottage country.

There is one more stop on our tour of Stoney Lake. Drive west on Highway 36 and south on Highway 28 to reach Young's Point. The Old Bridge Inn is a delightful stop for lunch, not only because of its historic appeal (the building dates to 1860), but also because of its site right beside the river. Lock 27 of the Trent–Severn Waterway, the rapids on the river, and Clear Lake are visible from the shaded, daylily-bordered patio and from the dining room. Hot and cold sandwiches, quiche, steak-and-kidney pie, chicken vol-au-vent and an assortment of homemade fruit pies are sure to please.

The original roadway bridge is now a pedestrian walkway that links the inn to a small park at Lock 27, a pleasant enough locality all on its own, but made even better by the Lockside Trading Company. This classic little white cottage was constructed in the 1850s as the first home at Young's Point. It was also the home of the Stoney Lake Navigation Company, which operated the steamboats described on the cruise. The cottage is an optical illusion: it looks small on the outside, but there's room after room of shopping fun on the inside. There are lots of country decorating accessories, such as afghans, tinware, decoys, antiques, Tilley Endurables, binoculars and paddles. Try the ice-cream cabin for something refreshing as you supervise the fisherfolk at the riverside.

One day on the shores of Stoney Lake surveys a broad sweep of history, from centuries-old petroglyphs, through quaint Victorian cottages, to a modern resort such as Viamede. Clearly, Stoney Lake has always been the place to be, then and now.

Petroglyphs Provincial Park
May–mid-October:
Daily 10–5
(705) 877-2552

Stoney Lake Cruises
(705) 652-8389

Viamede Resort
(705) 654-3344

Old Bridge Inn
(705) 652-8507

47 COBOURG
Putting Cobourg on the Map

Cobourg is one of those towns whose residents burst with civic pride, determined to keep their home locale in the public eye. They have done so for a couple of centuries, and in the process have created a community with grand architecture and a fine harbour.

Exit the 401 and drive right downtown to the main street, King Street. You can get to the historic harbour area, south of King Street, along either Third or Division Streets. There was no natural harbour here 160 years ago, but local settlers were determined to compensate for nature's oversight, and constructed excellent breakwaters and piers. Cobourg's harbour thus became an important centre for shipping, shipbuilding and yachting. The harbour is popular today with Great Lakes recreational boaters and with walkers who enjoy the boardwalk that leads to the beach and bandshell at Victoria Park.

From the harbour and Victoria Park walk north to King Street and turn west (left). Continue along to Cobourg's pièce-de-résistance, Victoria Hall. This very grand Palladian building expresses the optimism of mid-nineteenth-century Cobourg. It was built between 1856 and 1860, a time when Cobourg was competing with Toronto and Kingston to be the economic and political heart of the province. Kivas Tully designed the classical sandstone edifice with massive columns, pediments, a speaker's balcony, and elaborate decoration heavy with imperial symbolism. The building is crowned with a cupola and four-faced clock-tower. Best of all,

 Victoria Hall is set back from the street, which allows for a large civic square that is especially appealing when decorated for Christmas.

Victoria Hall's interior is equally impressive, with a spacious foyer tiled in black and white, a sunken courtroom, two grand staircases, and a breathtaking ballroom. Visitors are free to wander

through the hall and view the courtroom, and may ask at the municipal offices (to the left of the foyer) to see the ballroom and the main-floor office of Father of Confederation James Cockburn.

Don't miss the sunken courtroom, used as a provincial court on Mondays and Thursdays; at other times it is possible to see in through the doorway. The courtroom was modelled after the Old Bailey in London, and its appearance of severity and simplicity has changed little over the years.

The upstairs concert hall has been rightly named one of the grandest rooms in Canada. Those lofty ceilings may look like they are covered with ornate plasterwork, but those are clever trompe-l'oeil paintings. The walls are also lavishly decorated, just as they were when Prince Edward partied here all night to celebrate the opening of Victoria Hall in 1860. To this day, the hall remains at the heart of civic life here, as it is the home of several local and touring performing arts groups, and still serves as an impressive setting for civic and private functions.

The upper floor of Victoria Hall houses the Art Gallery of Northumberland, which hosts changing displays of local and national artists.

Exit the grand foyer and walk or drive west along King Street to number 212. This Regency cottage built in the mid-1800s is a redbrick heart-warmer with its diminutive form, hip roof, shuttered and mullioned windows, and doorway with sidelights. It is best known as the birthplace of early Hollywood legend Marie Dressler (born Leila Koerber). Now the home of the local Chamber of Commerce, it has several rooms devoted to Dressler's memory. Any movie fan will have a very interesting time examining the photographs, biographical information and replicas of the set of *Min and Bill*, which garnered Dressler an Oscar. Chamber of Commerce staff provide a brief but informative tour of the Dressler exhibits, and will play a biographical video.

Cobourg's residential areas are a showcase of historic architecture. You should be sure to set aside the time for a walking tour (brochures available at the Chamber of Commerce). Visitors who wish to prolong the historic mood should head for the Woodlawn Terrace Inn on Division Street for a fine meal. Woodlawn was built in 1835 for local businessman and civic founding father Ebenezer Perry. Like Dressler House, this is a Regency structure with hip roof and tall chimneys, but on a much grander scale. The interior decor emphasizes the elegance of the home, with period antiques and reproductions throughout. The menu features prime rib, seafood and pasta, as well as a variety of appetizers and desserts. The whole picture is so charming that you may decide to stay the night in the inn.

The harbour, Victoria Hall and Marie Dressler have all worked to put Cobourg on the map. Be a smart daytripper and put it on your map of places to visit soon.

Victoria Hall
Hours vary according to court
schedule
(905) 372-4301

Art Gallery of Northumberland
Tuesday–Friday 10–5
Saturday & Sunday 1–5
(905) 372-0333

Marie Dressler House
September–June:
Monday–Friday 9–5
Saturday 9–2
July & August:
Daily 9–5
(905) 372-2411

Woodlawn Terrace Inn
(905) 372-2235

48 CAMPBELLFORD
Countryside Rambles

Ever had one of those days when the job jar is empty, there's a clear blue sky overhead and the open highway beckons? A perfect day to head for the countryside around Campbellford, on the lower reaches of the Trent–Severn Waterway, for some flea-market bargains and backroad drives. Exit the 401 at Highway 30 and drive north.

 This region has a long history of dairy farming, a way of life going back to the United Empire Loyalists of the late 1700s. The verdant pastures are home to thousands of Holsteins, and the farms are prosperous and well-kept. At County Road 29 turn west to Warkworth, which has its own cheese factory just north of the village proper. There you'll find a tasty array of locally made cheddar, brick, mozzarella and Monterey Jack. The Northumberland Trading Company on the main street of Warkworth is a good place to put together a tailgate picnic; it offers unusual and wholesome soups, salads and sandwiches. Return to Highway 30 and continue the journey north.

Bargain hunters will hit the brakes at the Meyersburg Flea Market, which is open every weekend, year-round. This is a true, delightfully disorganized flea market, where stalls fill two barns and a parking lot, and where vendors hawk jewellery, mustard dispensers, clothes (a dollar per item), fresh eggs and vegetables, wrench sets and hammers (antique and new), phonograph records (remember vinyl?), weather vanes, dolls and toys. The book selections are good for those who love to hunt down encyclopedia sets or Boy Scout manuals from decades ago.

 Upon entering the southern section of Campbellford, look for signs directing travellers to the small park at Locks 11 and 12. The park is perfect for a picnic and a review of flea-market purchases. These locks are one of the two sets of hydraulic "flight" locks remaining on the Trent–Severn system; they are filled and emptied by gravity, and permit boats to climb a water staircase. The elevation overcome by these locks is huge, something appreciated only by peering down into the deep-dark lock when the water is at its lowest level. A display board in the park describes lock construction (the original log gates are still in use), operation (by hand winch), and maintenance (by diving crew).

Drive into Campbellford along Trent Drive. If the bargain hunter is not yet sated, there is flea market at 20 Trent that is similar to Meyersburg's, but with a greater emphasis on mechanical items such as machine-shop tools and equipment.

Campbellford has a lovely downtown with several historic buildings. The Town Hall is on River Street, and behind the Town Hall lies the Campbellford Farmers' Market (Saturdays during the summer). Also backing onto the market is the Mill House tearoom; its offerings of cream teas, pasta and salad, and amaretto and Black Forest cheesecakes are recommended for lunch.

Shoppers in the know head for two locations in town. The first, the Townsend Gallery, is at the corner of Doxsee and Second Streets. (From the market area, head south on Front to find Second Street, and walk east one block). This postcard-pretty 1886 home has been converted entirely to gallery space, and has a framing centre in a rear addition. The gallery has a huge selection of paintings by well-known artists such as Townsend, Romance, Saunders, Lumbers, Danby and Dumas. Further along Second Street is Campbellford's second claim to fame, World Class Chocolate — you can locate it blindfolded by following the luscious aroma. There is a retail sales shop on the premises (open Monday to Friday), and when that is not open, try Coxwell Gifts on Bridge Street for six varieties of individually wrapped chocolates and bars.

Historians will be interested in the Campbellford–Seymour Heritage Centre at 113 Front Street. This little rubblestone building was constructed in 1857 to serve as the Seymour Township Hall, and has since been used variously as jail, market, church and courtroom. Changing displays focus on local events and citizens, making this museum a treasure chest for anyone doing genealogical research in the region.

Enticing roads fan out from Campbellford in two directions. County Road 50 leads north to Healey Falls, a favourite haunt of geologists, who flock here to see where two different rock systems, the Trenton and Black River limestones, meet. The falls are also favoured by the rod-and-line crowd, and since the water is extremely shallow mid-summer, the exposed rocks are a popular wading spot. To the southeast, County Road 8 leads to the drumlin field of Ferris Provincial Park, or to Locks 8 and 9 (signs indicate a turn to Meyer's Lock), which are connected by a short trail. Bird-watchers will want to keep their eyes peeled for an osprey on its nest next to the canal and for shy Virginia rails in the riverside marshes.

When those rural roads call your name and you can't wait to head off into the hills, Campbellford and area are ready and waiting with plenty of rewarding countryside rambles.

Meyersburg Flea Market & Antiques
Saturday & Sunday 10–5
Also, mid-May–September:
Friday 10–5
(705) 653-3979

Campbellford–Seymour Heritage Centre
For information call
(705) 653-1551

49 BRIGHTON
The Apple of Our Eye

Apples are as integral to Ontario as maple syrup, Muskoka chairs, and campfires. Settlers from across Europe brought their own distinctive varieties of apple seedlings to their hard-won farmsteads, and the world's most popular apple, the MacIntosh, was developed in Eastern Ontario. To this day, apple harvest is a special time of year, one last chance to enjoy blue skies and crisp air before the snow flies.

A great place to participate in that apple harvest is in and around the orchards of Brighton. (Exit the 401 at Highway 30 southbound.) Take this trip any time from mid-August to mid-October. The last weekend of September is reserved for Applefest, when the streets are closed for a parade, sidewalk vendors, wagon rides, an amusement park and other activities.

It seems that every highway and byway around Brighton has dozens of roadside apple-stands. Signs tell which varieties are currently available, and the choice can seem mind-boggling: Melba, Rhode Island Greening, Gravenstein, St. Lawrence, Tolman Sweet, and Delicious are just a few of the many. The vendors are very knowledgeable and are happy to provide advice on the type of apples best suited for fresh eating, applesauce, baking, pickling, jellies and so on.

The largest farm market is at Rundle Farms on Highway 2, just west of Brighton (open daily, year-round). The entrance area has an array of straw people, corn stalks and pumpkins. There are bushels, baskets and crates of shiny apples, apple butter, hot and cold cider, juices, applesauce and even apple chips. Pumpkins and gourds come in a multitude of sizes, colours and shapes, from big, bumpy, green-and-yellow striped to small and white, and dark, smooth and round. Rundle's also sells other fall fruit, deli cheese and meat.

On the way into Brighton from Rundle Farms, stop in at Meadow Farm for a pick-your-own experience. The trees are semi-dwarf, which makes for easy, rapid picking, without the need for ladders for even the smallest child. In no time baskets and bags will be brimming with Paulared, MacIntosh, Empire or Idared. Travellers who arrive later in October will want to pick some golden brown, juicy Russets, which have a delectable aroma and taste.

Head into Brighton and follow signs to Proctor House Museum at 96 Young Street. Proctor House is an Italianate redbrick house with long, rounded windows and black shutters; it was built in the 1860s for John Edward Proctor, member of a large and very successful business family. The Proctor empire included mills, farms, stores, a hotel and a large Great Lakes shipping company. They ran a family orchard on this property until the 1930s.

Proctor House is for antique lovers, and its delights include Jacques & Hayes chairs, an 1850 Victorian love seat finished in needlepoint, a rug produced by six weavers over three years, and an 1870 grand piano. The library has a good collection of old Bibles, several encyclopedia, and a framed 1823 deed written on sheepskin. The kitchen, pantry and bedrooms are also furnished to period. No tour is complete without a climb to the rooftop cupola for a commanding view of crimson maples and scarlet sumach, Lake Ontario and Quinte's Isle. Proctor House staff host special events year-round, and during Applefest serve apple pie and cider on the back porch.

If the beautiful furnishings at Proctor House have you in the buying mood, drive to downtown Brighton and Richardson Street (parallel to Main Street and a few blocks south), the location of the Antique Warehouse. The scene at the entrance may well make you gasp with pleasure. A deeply carved walnut armoire, an oak and red leather partner's desk, a mint-condition roll-top desk, a weather-vane horse, a pine harvest table, and a mirror in a frame fit for a king — and that's just the first glance. This is a wonderful collection at good prices.

Look for smaller pieces and country-style decorations right next door at the Country Shop.

Drive along Highway 2 about 5 kilometres to tiny Smithfield. The main purpose here is to visit the Sap Bucket tearoom. Daily specials such as chicken-and-broccoli divan or crab quiche broaden the menu of soup and sandwiches, and during Applefest a serving of apple crisp and ice cream is de rigueur. The Sap Bucket is also a satisfying place for gift shopping, with the best in pottery, pewter, glass and linen for the bath, kitchen or dining room. There are also kids' books and games, collector plates and a year-round Christmas selection. Smithfield is also home to Heart to Heart Country Crafts, just down the street from the Sap Bucket, and the Smithfield Antique Gallery, around the corner on Smith Street.

Apple harvest season is a great time to gather up the entire family for a fresh-air outing in Brighton. And a little post-outing work in the kitchen can make that sweetness last the whole winter.

Proctor House Museum
July & August:
Monday–Friday 10–4
Saturday & Sunday 1–4
During Applefest weekend:
Daily 10–4
(613) 475-2144

50 PRESQU'ILE PROVINCIAL PARK
Fall Fling

When autumn brings crisp, dry weather to Ontario, all nature takes the opportunity to get busy and prepare for the chill winds of winter. Squirrels fill food caches, ducks and geese socialize and organize for the move to Florida, and groundhogs ready their homes for the long snooze. Daytrippers, too, feel the urge to be active and enjoy some outdoor fun. No better place than Presqu'ile Provincial Park, on Lake Ontario just south of Brighton.

 Presqu'ile is a spit, a sandy thumb sticking out into Lake Ontario. It owes its popularity among naturalists to two factors: habitat diversity and a unique location on the northern shore of Lake Ontario. The varied habitat types here include a large marsh, sand and pebble beaches, old fields, maple-beech forest, and northern, cedar forest. This diversity accounts for the fact that over 300 species of birds have been spotted here. Presqu'ile's location means that each fall, large flocks of waterfowl, land birds and Monarch butterflies rest and feed here before taking off on their long journey south.

The Monarch migration begins in August. The butterflies are hesitant to fly over the hazardous lake waters and hang around Presqu'ile until strong north winds provide good launching conditions. At peak migration, usually in late August, about 10,000 Monarchs can be seen massed on trees and shrubs at Owen Point (halfway along the western shore) or at Lighthouse Point (at the very end of the peninsula). Naturalists give talks on the Monarchs several weekends in late August and early September. Phone the park ahead of time to determine the progress of migration in order to plan your trip.

Bird migration takes place over a longer period of time. There are shorebirds in August, woodland birds and ducks in September, and hawks in October. There are several good observation points for fall bird-finding. There's the causeway near the entrance to the park; be alert for coot, gallinule and many species of ducks. Owen Point is the place to watch for migrating hawks. The Marsh Boardwalk Trail is a short hike through the cattails, where marsh wrens pop out to call at intruders and thousands of swallows roost each evening in August. The beaches along the western shore of Presqu'ile, busy with swimmers and sailboarders all summer, become important staging areas for sandpipers, plovers, gulls and terns. In fact, it is the beaches that garner the most excitement among visiting bird-watchers. American oystercatcher, curlew and stilt sandpipers, and American avocet are some of Presqu'ile's more interesting visitors.

Lakeshore Drive and Paxton Drive make a loop around the end of the peninsula. Lakeshore Drive is a good vantage point for viewing wintering ducks, including king eider, from September on. Paxton's route passes through prime woodland for migrating warblers. Park roadways are uncrowded in the fall, and the level terrain and decreased traffic make bicycling an excellent way to enjoy the park.

A new marine heritage centre is located in the original lighthouse-keeper's cottage at the very tip of the park. At the visitor centre you can find out about guided hikes, waterfowl-viewing weekends, stargazing and butterfly banding. The centre is also devoted to the human history of the park, which is every bit as intriguing as its wild side. The centre profiles characters such as Ben Kerr, "King of the Great Lakes Rumrunners," last seen in a boat heading for the American side in 1929; Ben Johnson, pirate during the War of 1812; and events such as the 1804 sinking of the schooner *Speedy*, with a full load of lawyers, witnesses and a murder suspect on board.

Take the time to explore Lighthouse Point, a promising place for a brown-bag lunch. This lighthouse, the second oldest still in operation on the Great Lakes, dates to 1840. As you soak up the last, bittersweet rays of sunshine you may notice that the waves have already turned from blue to the cold grey-green of winter. Still, the fresh sea breezes and the rhythm of the waves are therapeutic, and the view of offshore islands and fishing boats relaxing.

 There's one more activity left, and that is a walk in Jobe's Woods, a mature forest of maple, beech and hemlock. A 1-kilometre trail is located off Paxton Drive. Autumn in Jobe's Woods brings not only the vivid colours of maples, but also the orange and bronze of mushrooms and fungi. Those with eyes keen for one last look at a green landscape will want to search for the ferns of Jobe's Woods in rich, thigh-deep groves under the shade of tall trees; they stay a vivid colour until the killing frosts. The trail is very quiet now that the visitors of summer have departed, and you'll likely have the woods to yourself.

Autumn is a terrific time for heading outdoors to take in the last glow of warm weather and observe nature's busy preparations for winter. Make Presqu'ile your destination for a final fall fling.

Presqu'ile Provincial Park
Open daily, year-round
(905) 475-2204

BIBLIOGRAPHY

Information on tourist attractions came from many sources. Government publications and brochures printed by public and private facilities are too numerous to mention, but the following published sources deserve recognition.

Brown, Ron. *Backroads of Ontario*. Edmonton: Hurtig, 1984.

Brown, Lindsey. *The Bruce*. Tobermory: The Mariner Chart Shop, undated.

Brown, Lorraine. *The Trent–Severn Waterway. An Environmental Exploration*. Peterborough: Friends of the Trent–Severn Waterway, 1994.

Chandler, Margaret Ross. *The Great Little Country Inns of Southern Ontario*. Toronto: Deneau, 1989.

Perkins, Mary Ellen. *Discover Your Heritage. A Guide to Provincial Plaques in Ontario*. Toronto: The Ontario Heritage Foundation, 1918.

Pryke, Susan. *Explore Muskoka*. Erin: The Boston Mills Press, 1987.

Snowdon, Annette. *Discover Southern Ontario*. Toronto: Irwin Publishing, 1985.

Teasdale, Shirley. *Hiking Ontario's Heartland*. Toronto: Whitecap Books, 1993.

Wegg, Telfer. *Rural Routes. Exploring the Back Roads of Saugeen Country*. Neustadt, Ontario: T. Wegg Photography, 1994.